We thought this little book
would be a good one to
pick up and enjoy now
and then. Hope it brings
back some very happy
memories of Cork.

Lots of love,

Mike, Triona

& the gang!

x xx

THE
LITTLE
BOOK
OF
CORK

KIERAN McCARTHY

The
History
Press
Ireland

*Dedicated to those who stop
and say hello on Cork's streets*

First published 2015, reprinted 2016

The History Press Ireland
50 City Quay
Dublin 2
Ireland
www.thehistorypress.ie

The History Press Ireland are a member of Publishing Ireland,
the Irish Book Publisher's Association.

British Library Cataloguing in Publication Data.
A catalogue record for this book is available from the British Library.

ISBN 978 1 84588 875 6

Typesetting and origination by The History Press

Printed and bound by TJ International Ltd.

CONTENTS

ACKNOWLEDGEMENTS

Thanks to the staff of Local Studies of Cork City Library, Cork City and County Archives and Cork City Museum for their patience in dealing with so many of my queries over the past twenty years. Thanks to History Press Ireland for their experience and professionalism with this book.

INTRODUCTION:
BUILT ON A SWAMP

Cork City's growth on a swamp is an amazing story. The city is constructed on a shift-shaping landscape – sand and gravel, rushes and reeds – a wetland knitted together to create a working port through the ages. It also provides the foundation for the multifaceted narratives that tie this place together. There is a huge depth to this city's development. It was a combination of native and outside influences, primarily people who shaped its changing townscape and society since its origins as a settlement. The city possesses a unique character derived from a combination of its plan, topography, built fabric and its location on the lowest crossing point of the River Lee as it meets the tidal estuary and the second largest natural harbour in the world. Indeed, it is also a city that is unique among other Irish cities: it is the only one that has experienced all phases of Irish urban development, from around AD 600 to the present day. There is a very diverse set of archive and library records, some of which are very complete and some which are very fractious. Hence there are many diverse public spaces, historical structures and characters listed in this book.

Standing in the city's central Bishop Lucey Park, for example, are multiple monuments – remnants of the town walls, the arches for the old Corn Market gates (once behind City Hall), the smiling shawlie within Seamus Murphy's statue, and the swans of the fountain representing Cork 800. The fountain was placed there in 1985, a nod to the city's celebration of 800 years since the city's first charter in 1185. Then there is the imposing sinking tower of Christ Church and its ruinous graveyard. There is the ghostly feel of the buildings that once stood at the park's entrance. Along the latter stretch, living memory has recorded Jennings furniture shop, destroyed by fire in 1970; the toy shop of Percy Diamond who was cantor (a singer of liturgical music) at the Jewish synagogue; and the Fountain Café over which the famous hurler Christy Ring had a flat for a time. Of course when I mention just these strands, there are other layers I have not mentioned. The layered memories at times and their fleshed-out contexts are endless and often seem timeless.

The presence of all these monuments in the park often plays with my own mind on my walking tours – there is so much one can show and say. These urban spaces seem to slide between the past and present, between material and symbolic worlds. The mural by Mayfield Community Arts on the gable end of the shop next door to the park, entitled 'connecting our imagination, how do we imagine a positive future' is apt. The past does play on the imagination; it interconnects between spaces and times into our present and future. Memories flow and bend across the story of the development of this North Atlantic big hearted small city.

The displayed lower sections of the town walls are from the thirteenth century. During its excavation shards of pottery from Normandy, from the Saintonge region of France, from England, and from other parts of Ireland were also found during the excavation of the wall. For nearly 500 years (1170s to 1690), the town wall symbolised the urbanity of Cork and gave its citizens an identity within the town itself. The walls served as a vast repository of symbolism, iconography and ideology and as symbols of order.

The former town walls like this city were rebuilt in parts by inhabitants through hundreds of years. The river and the tide eroded at their base taking away the various sandstone and limestone blocks and perhaps re-shaping the more resistant ones. The surviving section in Bishop Lucey Park invites the visitor to reflect on life and resistance within the town and how layered the city's story is. There is wear and tear on the stones presented, which cross from the era of the walled town to the modern city. It invokes the imagination and if anything the wear and tear on our built heritage allows our minds to wonder and reflect on the life and times of people of the past and offers us ideas to take into our future world.

This book begins by delving into the multiple phases of Cork's development, its tie in to wider Irish history and to a degree how Cork branded itself through the centuries. From the creation of the first port, the city's coat of arms, to building international confidence as one of the self-proclaimed Venices of Northern Europe, Cork's historical development and ambition knew no bounds! However, certainly colonists such as the Vikings and Anglo-Normans and immigrant groups (and eventually citizens in their own right) such as Huguenots and Quakers led the settlement to have a role in the wider North Atlantic trade and beyond. All were involved in physically altering the townscape, constructing new buildings and quays and improving the interface with the river and the sea. Some key events such as Cork's role in the Irish War of Independence in the early twentieth century also led to changes to the city's fabric. The Burning of Cork incident led to many of its main street buildings, City Hall and Library being destroyed. The city rose from the ashes with a rebuild plan plus also strategies for the growing population and their requests for new housing areas.

Section 2 focuses on the array of public spaces and buildings that the city possesses. You can get lost in and around the multiple narrow streets and broad thoroughfares. Every corner presents the visitor with something new to discover. The pigeon-filled medieval tower of the Augustinian Red Abbey and the ruinous room of an old Franciscan well are rare historical jigsaw pieces that have survived the test of time. The dark dungeon at Blackrock Castle, with its canon opes, dates back to 1585 whilst the star-shaped structure of Elizabeth Fort has stonework stretching way back to the early seventeenth century. The city does not have much eighteenth century built heritage left. What does exist such as the Queen Anne 'Culture House' on Pope's Quay, represents an age where Dutch architecture was all the rage. A high pitched roof and elaborate and beautiful brickwork combines to make a striking structure. The legacy of the city's golden age of markets is present in the English Market, written about and critiqued since 1788.

Many architects have come and gone over the centuries but the rivalry of The Pain Brothers and the Deane family in the early nineteenth century inspired both families to excel in the design of some of the most gorgeous stone-built buildings from banks to churches to the quadrangle of University College Cork (UCC). All were embellished with local limestone, which on a sunny day, when the sun hits such a stone, lights up to reveal its splendour and the ambition of Ireland's second city. The settlement is also a city of spires linking back 1,400 years to the memory of the city's founding saint, Finbarre. The old medieval churches of St Peter and Christ Church are now arts centres but many of elements of their ecclesiastical past can be glimpsed and admired. Couple these with the beautiful St Anne's church tower and the scenery from the top of its pepper pot tower, the nineteenth-century splendour of the spires and stained glass of St Fin Barre's Cathedral and the sandstone block work of SS Mary's and Anne's North Cathedral, and the visitor can get lost in a world of admiration and wider connections to global religions. Then there is the determination that led the city to also possess the longest building in Western Europe – the old Cork Lunatic Asylum or Our Lady's Hospital and the tallest building in the country – County Hall, and only in recent years surpassed by the Elysian Tower.

Then there are the buildings which belong to the people. The current City Hall, the second building on the site, is the home of Cork City Council, formerly Corporation, which was established in Anglo-Norman times. The building is a memorial to the first building, which burned down in 1920, and to the memory of two martyred lord mayors, Terence McSwiney and Tomás MacCurtain. Terence died on a hunger strike and Tomas was shot in his house in Blackpool, both dying for the Irish War of Independence cause. The train station, Kent Station, also links through its name to Irish Easter Rising martyr, Tomas Kent. The station is the last of six railway stations, which travelled out into the far reaches of County Cork.

Cork's ambition was also displayed and carried by its people – its famous sons and daughters, who are explored in section three. Cork can boast connections to the wider world through its artists, architects and sculptors. They were renowned in their day, not just in Ireland but wider afield. Artists like James Barry and Daniel Maclise brought their own unique style into Britain's art worlds and galleries. Sculptors like John Hogan's and later

Joseph Higgins and Seamus Murphy inspired a generation of artists to take up their own artistic endeavours and created an international audience who wanted to see their work.

Here is a city as well that brought forward great writers of international standing such as Denny Lane, Daniel Corkery, Seán O'Faoláin, Frank O'Connor, and Seán Ó Riordáin. Composers range from Seán O'Riada to Aloys Fleischmann. Rory Gallagher, the famous electric guitar star of his day, is also remembered and his legend recalled regularly. Dancing into memory is the great ballet dancer and director Joan Denise Moriarty.

Amongst the city's eminent list of social reformers are Nano Nagle, Mary Aikenhead, Thomas Dix Hincks, Fr Theobald Mathew, Fr Christy O'Flynn and Br James Burke. All sought to help the city's impoverished. Amongst the remembered political leaders is Jack Lynch who became the city's only Taoiseach or Irish Prime Minister. Then there are the local heroes who gave the citizens employment, promoted freedom of expression, and above all showed that Cork is well able to fight for its position as Ireland's southern capital.

I have often walked around Cork in an attempt to get lost in its hidden corners, to be a tourist in my city, reading clues from bye-gone ages. The city does remember historical events which section four attempts to explore – the enormous temperance campaign of Fr Mathew is immortalised in his statue on St Patrick's Street, the National Monument commemorating Irish struggles against the British Empire before Independence. The First World War memorial on the South Mall is nestled into a nice green area and is set against the backdrop of the boardwalk.

However, weaving in and out of side streets and laneways, the visitor can get lost in the world of historical tales. Check out the city's former Mayoral House, a street made for a corn-market, a graveyard for deceased sailors, stories of steamships, educational morals in an art gallery, casts from the Vatican Art Gallery and tales of immigrants and their experiences from other parts of the world. Cork can boast to have a National Sculpture Factory in an old tramway engine house, colourful Harry Clarke windows, a former nineteenth-century waterworks made into a science centre, and an old famine relief project road, which turned into the site of world record motorcycle speed test attempt in the early twentieth century.

There is an underbelly to Cork's history as revealed in section five. It's a city where its ambition was pushed forcefully through takeover and colonisation. One image that always strikes me are the heads on spikes in the 1575 Pacata Hibernia map of the city. As a centre of power it created tensions between those who lived within its walls and those outside. Eventually the strength of the walled town succumbed to attack by Irish and Jacobite forces and in turn they were attacked and the city heavily damaged. Out of that event and an enlarging economy and population came crime in abundance. Many crimes were attempts to attain food for impoverished families. Watchmen patrolled the city's area where most offences occurred. Many were interred in Cork City Gaol. The more malicious criminals such as murderers and anti-crown supporters were hung at Gallows Green off Bandon Road, one of the city's large southern approach roads.

A look at the working life of Cork in section six reveals a very busy city through the ages. From medieval craft-making to creating the largest butcheries in the island of Ireland, Cork citizens were dedicated to making the port of Cork the premier harbour in the North Atlantic. Cork possessed the largest brewery and butter market in the country, hence hosting large-scale employment and inspiring other businesses to root themselves in the city and region. In the twentieth century, the firms of Fords and Dunlops gave employment to thousands of Cork people whilst creating a production empire of tractors, cars, tyres and even golf balls!

Not everyone was involved in the economic boom. Life in the city for the poorer classes was a struggle as outlined in section seven. Built across a swamp, life was damp – the streets were flooded regularly by the river and the tide. Economic boom brought a population explosion. Those who were not successful in securing employment filled the hallways of the poor house of the House of Industry in Blackpool and later during the Great Famine years and beyond, the Cork Union Workhouse on Douglas Road. Many left from ships on Cork's quays bound for countries such as Great Britain and further afield such as America. The story of

Annie Moore and her adventure to the metropolis of New York is representative of hundreds of thousands of people who became part of Ireland's diaspora legacy.

Scattered across the city are several sites, which have entertained the combined masses over many centuries as showcased in section eight. Take a stroll at the Mardyke, the Marina, and the Lough – they are institutions in the southern city. Barracka and Buttera Bands seem to have been around for time immemorial, entertaining citizens since the nineteenth century. Grabbing a ticket and sitting in Cork Opera House, Everyman Palace, the Firkin Crane and the Granary, the visitor can see the depth of dramatic talent and an opportunity to see the citizen uniting to support music, drama and the wider arts. This section also takes a glance at two of Cork's oldest cinema sites, the Pavilion and Savoy. The ideas of creating a spectacle, Cork has always taken to heart. It can also boast of building show grounds, viewing towers, Turkish baths, and world fairs!

Section nine gives an overview of Cork's prowess in sport since the records began. From rowing on the River Lee to tennis, cricket to the ball games of Gaelic Irish football and hurling, rugby and soccer, the city excels in several sports to great success. The section explores the highs and lows of this success, charting the heroes of Cork sport, from the bowling prowess of Mick Barry to the exemplary hurling skills of Christy Ring, to soccer legend Roy Keane, track athletes like Sonia O'Sullivan and Rob Heffernan, to rugby legends such as Ronan O'Gara and Peter Stringer.

So much to see, so much to do – welcome to the 'real capital' of Ireland!

Kieran McCarthy, 2015

1

A CITY AND ITS PHASES

ST FINBARRE, PATRON SAINT OF CORK

A legend records that the origins of Cork City begins at the source of the Lee in the scenic Shehy Mountains at the heart of which lies the cherished pilgrimage site of Gougane Barra (Finbarre's rocky cleft). Cork City's patron saint, St Finbarre, reputedly established one of his earlier monasteries on an island in the middle of Gougane Lake. Legend has it that he then left to walk the river valley at the mouth of which he established the monastery at what is now the site of St Fin Barre's Cathedral in Cork City. His myth endures in the valley and it is the legacy of St Finbarre that gives the city and valley its core spiritual identity and an origins story. Across the valley, there are churches named after Finbarre and a number of memorials depicting the saint in churches in the form of stained-glass windows and statues.

There are several ways of spelling the saint's name, but Finbarre is the most common. His connection seems rooted in several religious sites across the Lee Valley from source (Gougane Barra) to mouth (Cork City). Finbarre's *Life* was initially composed in Latin and was then passed down along three principal lines, each resulting in a major revision of the original text. In all, Finbarre's *Life* survives in thirty-five manuscripts and twenty-one copies in early vernacular. Finbarre's written vernacular life has undergone little major change between its earliest and latest extant copies. These date respectively from about 1450 to 1874. Finbarre's original *Life* seems to have been composed, perhaps as part of a collection, in Cork

St Finbarre, depicted in stained-glass window in church of the Immaculate Conception, Farran, County Cork.

between AD 1196 and 1201, some twenty-five years after the arrival of the Normans in south Munster. This was a time of reform in the Catholic Church.

Finbarre's hermitage was located around the area of present-day Gillabbey Street. It grew to be an important religious centre in southern Munster, providing ecclesiastical services in the form of a church and graveyard, and secular services in the form of a school, hospital and hostel. The annals record that languages such as Latin were taught at the school and that it was one of the five primary sites in Ireland in terms of size and influence. Word quickly spread of the monastery's valuable contribution to society, and it became necessary to expand the site. Between AD 600 and 800, a larger hermitage was constructed east of the original site, on open ground now marked by St Fin Barre's Cathedral. It is believed that over the subsequent centuries this hermitage grew to a point where it extended along the northern district of the lough, and extended on both sides of Gillabbey Street and College Road about as far as the locality now occupied by University College Cork (UCC).

Around the year AD 623 St. Finbarre died at the monastery of his friend, St Colman, at Cloyne in east Cork. His body was returned to his hermitage and his remains were encased in a silver shrine. Here they remained until 1089 when they were stolen by Dermod O'Brien. The shrine and the remains have never been recovered. Legend has it that the location of his tomb is just to the south-east of the present cathedral, over-looked by the famous Golden Angel. St Finbarre's feast day is celebrated on 25 September. As the city's patron saint he is still greatly revered.

VICIOUS VIKINGS

All that is known of the first recorded attack on the monastery at Corcach Mór na Mumhan was that it occurred in AD 820 and that the most valuable treasures were plundered. It is also known that it was raided four to five times in the ensuing 100 years. The marshy environment would not have been entirely welcoming, but the Vikings nonetheless established a settlement or longphort here. We cannot be sure of the exact location of the Viking town, but it is known that in AD 848 a settlement called Dún Corcaighe (Fort of the Marshes) was besieged by Olchobar, King of Caiseal from north Munster. It is thought that it was located on an island, the core of which could be marked by South Main Street, an area that was developed in ensuing centuries by other colonialists. With this in mind, Dún Corcaighe would have been located strategically near the mature stage of the River Lee, and therefore would have controlled the lowest crossing-point of the river, whilst being sheltered by the valley sides. The Norse invaders established a maritime network with other Viking ports, namely those at Dublin, Waterford, Wexford, and Limerick.

The Viking presence in Corcach Mór na Mumhan was interrupted by invaders from Denmark around AD 914 who also
attacked other Viking towns in Ireland and gained control of
them. In Cork, these new invaders – the Danish Vikings – started
off by raiding the monastery on the hillside but soon turned
their attention to wealthier and more powerful Gaelic kingdoms
in Munster. The Danes decided to settle in Ireland. They took
over and adapted existing Norwegian bases and constructed
additional ones to a similar but larger design. Unfortunately,
the historical and archaeological information available regarding
a Danish settlement at Cork is poor compared to that arising
from excavations in Waterford and Dublin. Nevertheless, there
are some clues that give an insight into the location, structure
and society of Danish Viking-Age Cork. It is known that there
were at least three main areas of settlement: firstly, they lived
on the southern valley side next to the monastery, the core area
of which is present-day Barrack Street; secondly, they settled
on a marshy island now the location of South Main Street,
the Beamish and Crawford Brewery, Hanover Street and Bishop
Lucey Park; and thirdly they settled on the adjacent northern
valleyside, now the area of John Street in Lower Blackpool.

The publication *Archaeological Excavations at South
Main Street 2003-2005* (2014) records Hiberno Norse structures
found under South Main Street area. Two to three metres under-
neath our present-day city, archaeologists exposed the remains of
timber structures. The dendrochronological dates of the timbers
found on the site suggest that there was continuous felling of
trees and construction of buildings and reclamation structures
from just a few years before 1100 to 1160. So here on a swamp
900 years ago, a group of settlers decided to make a real go at
planning, building, reconstructing and maintaining a mini town
of timber on a sinking reed-ridden, riverine tidal space.

A SAFE HARBOUR FOR SHIPS

By the early 1170s the Anglo-Normans had taken control of large
tracts of land from Waterford to Dublin. In 1172 they turned their
attention to Cork. Two Anglo-Norman lords, Milo de Cogan

and Robert Fitzstephen, were despatched to Corcach Mór na Mumhan with a small land force to confront and dispossess the Vikings and chief of the McCarthys, Dermod McCarthy, of his lands in counties Cork and Kerry. Once they had been defeated, Fitstephen and De Cogan began the transformation of the settlement into an Anglo-Norman town. It was to become one of fifty-six early Anglo-Norman walled towns established in Ireland, some re-founded on adapted and extended Viking settlements sites. Initially, they noted that the Danish settlement on the marshy island was 'fortified' and had a gate (*'porta'*) leading into it. The nature of the fortification, whether it was stone or timber, was not recorded. Incorporating elements of the old settlement, the newcomers instigated many fundamental changes to the town.

The name of the town was shortened to Corke. The renaming was significant as it was the first instance of the anglicising of a Gaelic name. In the late 1100s, Henry II chose Bristol as the model to be followed in developing manorial towns in Ireland, especially in issues such as liberties, privileges and immunities. Corke was to have its own mayor, sheriffs, and a corporation of councillors. The city still possesses these legacies. The term is now Lord Mayor and the Corporation a City Council.

Between the 1170s and 1300s, a stone wall, on average 8 metres high, became the new perimeter fence for the old Viking settlement area on the island, which was accessible via a new drawbridge built on the site of the Viking bridge, Droichet. Beyond this wall, a suburb called Dungarvan (now the area of North Main Street) was established on a nearby island.

By 1317 the full circuit, which included the extension of the wall around Dungarvan, was complete. Thus the redevelopment of the town walls created one single walled settlement (6½ha. in extent) instead of a walled island with an unfortified island settlement and Dungarvan outside it. Within the town a channel of water was left between the old walled settlement and the newly encompassed area of Dungarvan, with access between the two provided by an arched stone bridge called Middle Bridge. A millrace dominated the western half of this channel, while the remaining eastern half was the town's central dock.

The wall had mural towers at regular intervals that projected out and were used as lookout towers by the town's garrison of soldiers.

The walled town extended from South Gate Bridge to North Gate Bridge and was bisected by long spinal main streets, North and South Main Streets. These were the primary routeways and although narrower than the current streets, would have followed an identical plan. They would also have been the main market areas.

The town was now well defended and all those seeking to gain entry had to use one of the three designated entrances: one of the

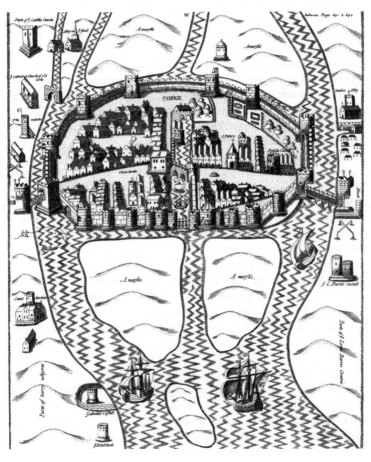

The walled town of Cork, as depicted in Sir George Carew's *Pacata Hibernia, or History of the Wars in Ireland*, vol. 2 (1633).

two well-fortified drawbridges with associated towers or the eastern portcullis gate. The first drawbridge, allowing access from the southern valleyside, was South Gate Drawbridge, while entry from the northern valleyside was via North Gate Drawbridge. From 1300 to 1690 these were the only two bridges spanning the River Lee. There are still bridges on these sites today and they still possess the names North and South Gate Bridge. The current South Gate Bridge dates to 1713 while the North Gate Bridge dates to 1961.

The third entrance overlooked the eastern marshes and was located at the present-day intersection of Castle Street and Grand Parade. Known as Watergate, it comprised a large portcullis gate that opened to allow ships into a small, unnamed quay located within the town. On either side of this gate, two large mural towers, known as King's Castle and Queen's Castle, controlled its mechanics.

The Anglo-Normans consolidated this port by establishing new export destinations and by the end of the seventeenth century, the walled town of Cork was exporting to other European ports such as to Bordeaux, in France, and to a large range of English Ports such as Bristol, Chichester, Minehead, Southampton and Portsmouth. Trading contacts were also made across the Atlantic Ocean to eastern North American ports such as Carolina and those in the Caribbean, trading goods such as beef and butter. In addition, the sheltered nature of the mature river valley and Cork harbour has provided a safe berth for ships right through the ages.

The coat of arms of the city comprises two battlemented towers with a ship, depicted as a medieval galleon, in between. The arms are said to depict King's and Queen's Castles, which operated Watergate. A Latin motto is attached: *Statio Bene Fida Carinis* (a safe harbour for ships).

A VENICE OF THE NORTH

For nearly 500 years (*c*.1200-*c*.1690), the walled port town of Cork remained as one of the most fortified and vibrant walled settlements in the expanding British colonial empire. However, economic growth as well as political events in late seventeenth-century Ireland, culminating in the Williamite Siege of Cork in 1690, provided the catalyst for large-scale change within the urban area. The walls were allowed to decay and this was to inadvertently alter much of the city's physical, social and economic character in the ensuing century.

By John Rocque's Map of Cork in 1759, the walls of Cork were just a memory – the medieval plan was now a small part in something larger – larger in terms of population (from 20,000 to 73,000) and in terms of a new townscape. A new urban text emerged with new bridges, streets, quays, residences and warehouses built to intertwine with the natural riverine landscape.

The 1759 map is impressive in its detail. John Rocque (c.1705-62) was a cartographer and engraver of European repute. He could count among his achievements maps of London, Paris, Berlin and Rome. The features that stand out on his Cork map are the canals and the links to changing technologies, reclamation, bridge construction, river bank consolidation, creation of quays – all linked to new emerging urban civilisation within a network of canals, reminiscent of Venice, Amsterdam, Copenhagen – Cork's central canal lined the centre of the newly reclaimed area, admirable buildings on both sides bearing a special relationship with the water. By 1790, many of these were to be filled, creating wide and spacious streets like St Patrick's Street, Grand Parade and the South Mall.

During the eighteenth century Cork gained the nickname the Venice of the North. It would be great to point to a myriad of real physical Venetian imagery and perspectives in eighteenth-century Cork but this terminology seems only to exist in the legacies of that time. Indeed it is more commented upon in nineteenth-century antiquarian books and late twentieth-century history books of Cork than in the traveloques of eighteenth-century antiquarians.

Economically, in the eighteenth century, the city was booming. By 1730, the population had increased to 56,000 and by 1790 it was 73,000. This was a large increase since a population of 20,000, 100 years previously in 1690. The settlement's harbour and hinterland maintained a lucrative provision trade. Cork's exports comprised on average 40 per cent of the total export from Ireland with just over 70 per cent of this total sent to the European mainland. The list of countries included; Denmark, Norway, Sweden, France, Germany, Great Britain and the coastal islands, Holland, Italy, Portugal, Spain, Barbadoes,

Turkey and Greenland. Cork held 80 per cent of the Irish export to England's American colonies. The main ports include Carolina, Hudson, Jamaica, Montreal, Quebec, New England, New Foundland, New York, Nova Scotia, Pennsylvania, Virginia, Maryland and the West Indies. Exports were also sent to New Zealand and the Canaries. By 1800, Cork was reputed to be the most noteworthy transatlantic port.

HUGUENOTS AND QUAKERS

The north-eastern marshes became a significant area of development for the Huguenot congregation in Cork. By the mid-1700s, over 300 Huguenots had established themselves in Cork City. Many of them worked as trades people, especially in the textile industry and in the manufacture of linen and silk. The Huguenots were also involved in property development and one of the first Huguenot families to develop property was Joseph Lavitt whose family were primarily involved in overseas trade and sugar refining and constructed Lavitt's Quay in 1704. The areas of present-day French Church Street, Carey's Lane and Academy Street in the city centre are located at the core of the Huguenot quarter with the name 'French Church' also reflecting their involvement in townscape change in Cork in the early eighteenth century.

To the west of the crumbling walled town, the religious group, the Quakers reclaimed and developed large portions of the marshy islands. This community had been in Cork since 1655, but it was only in the early 1700s that they were legally given the opportunity to develop their own lands.

The Quaker movement began in northern England around 1650 and developed out of religious and political conflict. Also known as the Religious Society of Friends, they were a breakaway group from mainstream Protestantism. With the presence of massive opportunities for trade, the Quakers established themselves in Cork City and in other Munster towns such as Bandon, Skibbereen, Charleville and Youghal.

One of the first Quaker pioneers in the development of the western marshes was Joseph Pike, who purchased marshy land in 1696, now the area of Grattan Street. Another key player was John

Haman, a respected linen merchant who also owned land in the northern suburbs. Minor players included the Devonshire family, the Sleigh family and the Fenn family (Fenn's Quay today marks their land). In the eastern marshes, a Quaker by the name of Captain Dunscombe bought land, now the area of the multi-storey car park on the Grand Parade and part of present-day Oliver Plunkett Street.

One noted Quaker, William Penn, spent much time in the Cork area. Born in 1644 in Tower Hill, London, William was the son of Admiral William Penn. Educated at Oxford, he was expelled for non-conformity, reputedly because of his contact with the Quaker movement. Subsequently, he went to France to study for two years at the Protestant University of Saumur, before returning to London to study law at Lincoln's Inn. In the 1650s, Oliver Cromwell gave his father a considerable estate, the castle and manor of Macroom in County Cork. On the accession of Charles II in the 1660s, he was dispossessed of this property and was compensated with lands in Shanagarry, County Cork. In 1667, his father sent him to manage the estate. While in east Cork, he was influenced by his friend, a Quaker, Thomas Lee and converted to Quakerism. William visited the walled town of Cork in 1667 and attended a Quaker meeting. William Penn went on to become a well-known author of a large number of literary books and pamphlets, which supported Quaker doctrines and eventually emigrated to America where he was very instrumental in establishing the State of Pennsylvania, which was named after him.

THE INTERNATIONAL CITY

One hundred years ago, considerable tonnage could navigate the North Channel, as far as St Patrick's Bridge, and on the South Channel as far as Parliament Bridge. St Patrick's Bridge and Merchants' Quay were the busiest areas, being almost lined daily with shipping. Near the extremity of the former on Penrose Quay was situated the splendid building of the Cork Steamship Company, whose boats loaded and discharged alongside the quay.

In the late 1800s, the port of Cork was the leading commercial port of Ireland. The export of pickled pork, bacon, butter, corn, porter, and spirits was considerable. The manufactures of the city were brewing, distilling and coach-building, which were all carried out extensively. The imports in the late nineteenth century consisted of maize and wheat from various ports of Europe and America; timber from Canada and the Baltic; fish from Newfoundland and Labrador regions. Bark, valonia, shumac, brimstone, sweet oil, raisins, currants, lemons, oranges and other fruit, wine, salt and marble were imported from the Mediterranean; tallow, hemp and flaxseed from St Petersburg, Riga and Archangel; sugar from the West Indies; tea from China, and coal and slate from Wales.

THE BURNING OF CORK

In December 1920, six unknown IRA men ambushed auxiliaries within a hundred metres of the central military barracks near Dillion's Cross in Cork City. Victoria Barracks, named after Queen Victoria, was originally built in 1806. During the 1920 ambush, empty lorries used to transport auxiliaries were bombed and auxiliaries themselves were raked with revolver fire. At least one auxiliary was killed and twelve others were wounded. In retaliation, the auxiliaries and Black and Tans commenced indiscriminate shooting in the main city centre streets shortly after eight o'clock. Curfew was at ten o'clock but long before that the streets became deserted. At ten o'clock two houses were set alight by the 'Tans' at Dillion's Cross and the adjacent roads were patrolled to prevent any extinguishing of the flames. Soon, petrol was brought into the city centre and various premises at random were set alight. No distinction was made between Loyalist and Nationalist premises.

The fires spread rapidly and soon most of the eastern portion of St Patrick's Street was blazing. In addition, the City Hall and the city's Carnegie Library were destroyed with the loss of large portions of Cork's public and historic records. The complete gutting of St Patrick's Street led to a full reconstruction within ten years and. However, a new City Hall was only built in the early 1930s. It was opened by Eamon De Valera in 1936.

TWENTIETH-CENTURY EXPANSION

The report *Cork, A Civic Survey* revealed that in 1925, around 80,000 people lived in Cork City and that 12,850 houses in the whole city were inhabited by 15,469 families. One ninth of the total population, nearly 9,000 families, were still living in tenements, with an average of twelve people in each house. The highest mortality rates were just north and north-west of the northern channel of river in Shandon and Blackpool. Many died of diseases such as diphtheria, scarlatina and typhoid. The suggested improvements involved re-housing on a massive scale. The 'Civic Survey' outlined that one fifth of the population, some 16,000 people, would have to be re-housed and the right sites would have to be found, along with the appropriate services and communications.

Alleviating the social problems existing in the city began immediately with new housing built in three main suburban areas. Firstly, in the southern suburbs of the city, the area of Turners Cross became quickly developed with Corporation housing and as a result, the area became a parish in 1927 and between the years 1928 to 1932, a new church named Christ the King was built in the area. The site chosen in the northern suburbs was Gurranabraher. Compulsory-purchase orders were enforced and the required land was obtained. The project also involved the demolition of many old cottages and the destruction of several laneways under a slum-clearance order. The initial phase of building comprised 354 dwellings. The first 200 houses were officially opened and blessed by the Catholic Cork Bishop Daniel Cohalan on 17 March, St Patrick's Day, 1934.

By the 1950s, shortage of building land for new housing estates meant more city suburbs such as Ballyphehane (south side) and Farranree (north side) began to be built. Nearly, 1,000 houses were constructed in Ballyphehane alone between 1948 and 1960. The Corporation also bought land in the city's southern suburbs, such as the Lough and Ballyphehane. Much of this land was used as market gardens to supply markets at Coal Quay and English Market. On the north side of the city, the lands known as Churchfield to the north of Gurranabraher were developed. In 1955, such was the extent of building in the suburbs that the Corporation decided to recognise the development outside the city boundary and, in conjunction with the county council, extended the municipal boundary by 346 hectares.

Cork Airport opened in 1961 and was Ireland's third airport after Shannon and Dublin. This development opened up further European markets and predictions in the early 1960s argued that 30,000 passengers per annum would be handled in the early years, reaching a target of 60,000 people per annum after five years. In fact, in that first year 75,000 passengers used the airport and this figure grew steadily to over 160,000 in 1967. Today, the passenger traffic of the airport exceeds 1.5 million per annum and continues to grow.

In the early 1970s the population of Cork City rose by a further 10,000 people. In 1978, a coherent overall plan was eventually published regarding the future of land use and transport in the city. Known as the Land Utilisation and Transport Study, or LUTS, its main goals have nearly all been completed. As part of LUTS, a downstream crossing was proposed and opened in May 1998 at the Lee Tunnel, or to give it its official title, the Jack Lynch Tunnel.

THE NEW MILLENNIUM

Twenty-first-century architecture is prominent in Cork; the front façades of the Cork Opera House and the Gate Cinema are two noteworthy examples. The first decade of the twenty-first century coincided with an overhaul of St Patrick's Street as a central urban space. Designed by Spanish architect Beth Gali, it is a central retail and business quarter, worthy of a European regional capital. Furthermore, the Cork Docklands Project, commissioned by Cork City Council, is working on a new urban quarter in Cork, a vibrant mix of residential and non-residential sites.

2

PUBLIC SPACES AND BUILDINGS

IN AND ABOUT THE CITY

Blackrock Castle
The citizens of Cork built Blackrock Castle in 1582 to safeguard ships against pirates who would come into the harbour to steal away their vessels. The fort, which was then a circular tower also had a turf fire so it could be used as a beacon light to guide shipping. In 1722, the old tower was destroyed by fire and a new one built by the citizens.

Blackrock Castle, 1863. (*Illustrated London News*)

In 1759, Admiralty Courts were held at Blackrock Castle. It was the court's job to organise an important ceremony called 'Throwing the Dart'. This was a rite by which the Mayor of Cork threw a metre long dart into the water of Cork Harbour in order to show his authority over the port and harbour. This is a function still carried out by the Lord Mayor of Cork.

In 1827, the second tower was also destroyed by fire. The rebuilding of the ancient castle commenced in 1828 and was completed on 3 March 1829. The current building has now been developed as a museum, exploring the history of the universe and Irish scientists and now boasts a state-of-the-art observatory on the site.

Elizabeth Fort

The star-shaped fortification of Elizabeth Fort, named after Queen Elizabeth I, once protected an English garrison in Cork and became a distinct landmark in the immediate southern suburbs of seventeenth-century Cork. Constructed in 1601, the fort protected the walled town of Cork from attack from Gaelic Irish natives and Spanish invasion. To enter into the original interior, one had to cross a drawbridge, go through a

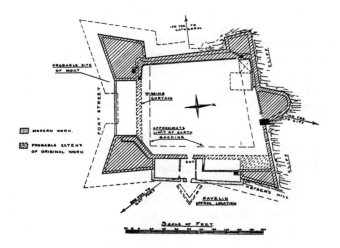

Plan of Elizabeth Fort.

portcullis gate and past a gatehouse. None of the original fort can be seen today.

In 1806, due to the construction of the 'New Barrack's' to the north east of the city (now Collins Barracks), the barracks within Elizabeth Fort was altered to that of a Female Convict Prison. In the late nineteenth century, the fort was used as a station for the Cork City Artillery Militia. In 1920-21, it was occupied by the Royal Irish Constabulary and handed over to the Provisional Irish Government. A year later in 1922, the interior buildings of the fort were burned down by Anti-Treaty forces but the walls and bastions of the fort were undamaged. A few years later, a Garda station was set up in the interior of the fort and today is still in operation.

Elizabeth Fort remains one of Cork's most historic gems. It has never been excavated – so a wealth of stories may still be waiting to be discovered.

Cork's Culture House

Built around 1730, the distinctive Queen Anne redbrick building on 50 Pope's Quay is unique not only to Cork but to Ireland and is very much a city landmark. It is believed to have been originally built for Richard Boyle, the 4th Earl of Cork. The house has undergone a number of uses through the centuries. It was occupied by a Master Cooper, Henry Maultby, until 1876, when the building was used as the County and City of Cork Hospital for Women and Children. In 1885, the hospital reverted to a cooperage. By 1907, Patrick Ryan, an RIC sergeant, and his family occupied the house, and at least two of his daughters – the building's last-known residents – lived there until the 1980s after which the building began to fall into dereliction.

In 1997, a restoration project commenced as a result of private business, Government, EU and Cork City Council support. However, restoration work ceased in 2000 due to a shortage of funds until the Musgrave Group came to the rescue in December 2002, sponsoring completion of the project to the tune of €450,000. The building embarked on a new chapter in its long history as the headquarters for the European Capital of Culture during 2005. It became a focal point during one of the most important periods in Cork's cultural history. It is now home to many of the city's festivals and their administration team.

The Pain Brothers

George Richard and James Pain began their career as apprentices to an architect named John Nash in London and afterwards established their own firm in Cork. They attained their interest from their father James, who was Director of the Society of Architects of Great Britain in 1771. On their arrival to Ireland, they settled down, George in Cork and James in Limerick. James managed to attain the position of architect for the Board of First Fruits for the province of Munster. Consequently, he was responsible for building, altering and repairing numerous churches dispersed throughout the province – creating substantial work for himself and his brother. Their principal works included churches at Buttevant, Midleton and Carrigaline. They introduced into the associated towers and spires, elements of their own architectural interests in the form of Gothic (pointed-arch) architecture. They also designed Mitchelstown Castle for the Earl of Kingston along with several large bridges in the Limerick area.

In Cork, George Pain was elected as a freeman of the city in 1827. Along with his brother, they completed a wide range of architectural work in the city and its environs. Their earliest work in the area was the Church of Ireland in Blackrock in

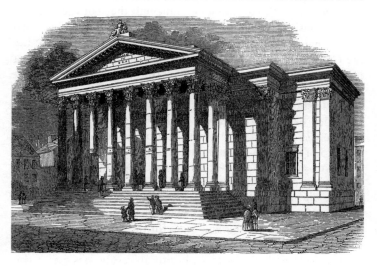

Cork City Courthouse, 1843. (*Illustrated London News*)

1819. They were responsible for the redesigning of St Mary's and St Anne's, North Cathedral and Blackrock Castle. Both interiors had been gutted by fire in the early 1820s. In addition, they were responsible for the design of Holy Trinity church (Catholic), St Patrick's church (Catholic) and St Luke's church (Anglican) and a new City Court House, all in the 1830s.

The Deane Intervention

The Deane family were natives of County Down but migrated south to Cork in the latter half of the 1700s. Alexander Deane was the first to encourage design and construction in the family. In 1790, he married Elizabeth, the daughter of Thomas and Elizabeth Sharp of Cork. They had five sons and three daughters but misfortune struck in 1806 when Alexander died at the age of 45. Thomas Deane, the eldest son of Alexander, took on the business. Born in 1792, his father died when he was fourteen. Under the influence of his mother, he educated himself and his brothers and sisters. Gaining a qualification in architecture, he went on to manage his father's business. Unlike the Deane dynasty that had gone before him, Thomas managed to carve out a very public career as a professional architect.

In the pre-Catholic emancipation era and at the age of 21 he was responsible for the design of the Commercial Buildings, later to become the Imperial Hotel on the South Mall in 1813 and the City Gaol, Shanakiel in 1824. In recent times, the gaol has been operated as a heritage centre. In time Deane became the city's principal architect. He was well respected in the city and this was shown in 1815 when he was appointed High Sheriff, an office bestowed on him again in 1830. Indeed, in 1830, he received a knighthood from the Lord Lieutenant of Ireland. In 1823, Thomas built Dundanion Castle as his own residence. This was a large mansion, which lay adjacent to a fifteenth-century tower house in Blackrock.

Other principal works include St Mary's Dominican church, Pope's Quay and the Trustee Savings Bank on Lapp's Quay. All the latter buildings had their foundation stones laid in the 1830s. Perhaps the most notable of their works was the Quadrangle of University College Cork. The design of this building was completed in association with another prominent architect, Benjamin Woodward, and opened in 1849. In 1852, The Deanes merged their business with Woodward and the firm became known as Sir Thomas Deane, Son & Woodward and opened an office in Dublin on Merrion Street.

The College

The origins of University College, Cork (UCC) dates to the early half of the 1800s. UCC was founded under the provisions made by Queen Victoria to endow new colleges in Ireland for the advancement of learning. Under the powers given by this act, the three colleges of Belfast, Cork and Galway were incorporated on 30 December 1845. Architects Benjamin Woodward and Sir Thomas Deane adopted a perpendicular Gothic style. The Cork college opened on 7 November 1849. In 1854, one of the college's most eminent professors was appointed, George Boole. A native of Lincoln in England, from an early stage in his life, he possessed an interest in mathematics. In 1844, Boole was awarded a gold medal by the Royal Society and developed a new branch of mathematics known as Boolean algebra.

In 1908, the Queen's College, Cork was established as a National University of Ireland under the 1908 constitution. Today, University College Cork has 12,000 students and 1,700 staff. It is located in a beautiful campus in the heart of Cork city. The college has always maintained a tradition of academic excellence across a wide range of disciplines. It has established a reputation as one of the top institutions in Ireland for innovative research in the humanities, sciences, engineering, medicine and business. Students come to UCC from over sixty countries to pursue their studies in a stimulating academic environment and to be part of a vibrant community sharing a rich social and cultural experience.

Provincial Bank

The earliest Cork bank was established by Quakers Edward and Joseph Hoare in the late 1600s. Private banks grew rapidly in the early 1800s, especially during the years of the Napoleonic Wars. Banks began to appear in many inland towns and smaller ports where no banks had previously existed. Between 1815 and

1835, the value of Irish exports rose by 33 per cent. One such influential banking institution, the Provincial Bank system, was founded between 1824 and 1836 and initially most of its original capital came from Britain, with its staff primarily Scottish people. By the 1860s, thirty-one branches were based in Munster. In 1878, the number of branches was 403.

The Cork building was constructed during the years 1863 and 1865 and was acclaimed on its opening in 1865 as the 'handsomest public building in Cork'. Costing between £15,000 and £20,000, it complemented the older Cork Saving Banks (est. 1832) on Lapp's Quay. Alex Deane, an uncle of Sir Thomas Deane, designed the white limestone building. The ground floor is faced with ashlar while the windows have a semi-circular heading and large niches are present on either side of the entrance. The Provincial Bank is now the property of Thomas Crosbie Holdings. Over the windows in the Parnell Place frontage of the former Provincial Bank are the arms of Sligo, Belfast, Cork, Dublin and Ireland. There are also limestone panels, which show commerce, industry, agriculture and shipping.

Justice, Law and Mercy

In 1829 it was decided by Cork Corporation that the City and County Courthouses should be incorporated into one building, to be located on Washington Street. Designed by George Pain, the Courthouse was opened in 1835. Years later, on Good Friday, 27 March 1891, the interior was completely destroyed by fire. William Henry Hill was chosen to oversee the reconstruction of the building and thirty-three months later, on 18 March 1895, the first rooms of the new and present Courthouse were opened for the Spring Assizes. In the middle of the twentieth century, to modernise the aesthetics of the building, the railings, which surrounded the building were removed and in more recent times, the interior of the Courthouse has been modernised and the exterior walls have been renovated.

The front of the building facing onto Washington Street possesses a noble Corinthian portico. The front range of Corinthian columns projects nearly 6 metres from the main building. The pillars are nearly 10 metres high. The group of figures, which stand over the building, represent justice, law and mercy.

The Market

The English Market was opened in 1788 and was known then as the Root Market. Today Corkonians know the market under several names: the Princes Street Market, the English Market, the Grand Parade market or some call it 'De Market'. By the mid-1800s, the market had fallen into a state of disrepair. In 1862 the market was rebuilt under the direction of architect Sir John Benson. The renovations were considered very successful.

The market has suffered two fires, one in 1980 and the other in 1986. After the 1980 fire, the market was again renovated at a cost of £500,000 and once again it was considered a great success, some of the original features were retained even. The fire of 1986 caused an estimated cost of £100,000 worth of damage. Nevertheless, the market was again repaired. A main feature of the market is the Market Fountain, which is a traditional part of market life. Despite being ornate, it was functional and it provided the market's water until Cork Corporation installed running water in the 1960s. A characteristic of the market is the selling of tripe and drisheen, which are both traditional foods and have been eaten in Cork for centuries. Drisheen is extra special as it is indigenous to Cork.

A Skyscraper to Catch the Eye

In 1898, the Local Government (Ireland) Bill had a rapid passage through the British Parliament resulting in new council structure of county, district and municipal. The new county councils would take over the administration and taxation duties of the Grand Juries at County Sessions. The first election for the Cork County Council took place on 6 April 1899. The term of office was three years.

Work began on a new City Hall for Cork County Council in 1965. It was designed by County Council Architect Patrick McSweeney and was officially opened by Martin Corry, TD, chairman of Cork County Council, on 16 April 1968. In recent times, County Hall has undergone an extension and redevelopment. An invited competition was organised by the Royal Institute of the Architects of Ireland and the management team at Cork County Council for the general refurbishment of County Hall. Today a total of fifty-five councillors, representing eight electoral divisions, serve the county. This is the largest elected assembly outside Dublin. County Hall tower is the tallest building in the Republic of Ireland and its foundations are 15m deep.

Ireland's Longest Building

Cork also boasts Ireland's longest building, just across the river from County Hall, in the shape of the Victorian Mental Hospital. It was originally named Eglinton Lunatic Asylum after the Earl of Eglington, and was opened in 1852. In the 1870s, three blocks were connected into a single building. In 1852, the principal types of people admitted comprised housewives, labouring classes, servants, and unemployed. Forty-two forms of lunacy were identified from causes such as mental anxiety, grief, epilepsy, death, and emigration to 'religious insanity', nervous depression, want of employment and desertion of husband or wife.

In 1952, the hospital's name was changed to Our Lady's Psychiatric Hospital. From the 1950s, the long grey limestone building was reorganised into wards and various units were renamed. The western side became known as St Ita's whilst the eastern side, the male ward, became known as St Patrick's. Our Lady's Psychiatric Hospital closed in the late 1980s and in recent years, parts of the main grey building have now been redeveloped into apartments.

PIECES OF ART

Red Abbey

The central bell tower of the church of Red Abbey is a relic of the Anglo-Norman colonisation and is one of Cork's last remaining visible structures, which dates from the era of the walled town. Invited to Cork by the Anglo-Normans, the Augustinians established an abbey in Cork, sometime between 1270 and 1288. The uncertainty of the date is due to an absence of records for this medieval order in Cork and the information we do possess primarily appears in the work of

Sir James Ware, an Elizabethan antiquarian who highlights the history of Red Abbey in his writings in 1658; '*De Hibernia et Antiquitatibus Eius*'. In addition, nineteenth-century Cork antiquarians such as John Windele in 1844 and Charles Gibson in 1861 relate in their publications on Cork, stories of archaeological discoveries and folklore about the area.

It is known that in the early years of its establishment, the Augustinian friary became known as Red Abbey due to the sandstone used in the building. It was dedicated to the Most Holy Trinity but had several names, which appear on several maps and depictions of the walled town of Cork and its environs. For example, in a map of Cork in 1545, it was known as St Austin's while in 1610, Red Abbey was marked as St Augustine's.

In the mid-eighteenth century, some of the buildings of Red Abbey were used as part of a sugar refinery. This refinery was accidentally burnt down in December 1799. Since then, the friary buildings, with the exception of the tower, have been taken down. The tower is maintained by Cork City Council who were donated the structure by the owners in 1951 and own other portions of the abbey site. Today, the tower of Red Abbey, which is approximately 30 metres high, is one of Cork's most important protected historic structures. The tower cannot be climbed but medieval architecture can still be seen on the lower arch of the structures and in the upper windows.

The Franciscan Well

In the twelfth and thirteenth centuries, a number of religious houses were established in the suburbs of the walled town of Cork. On the northern hillside, large tracts of land were owned by the Franciscans, who also established an associated abbey on what is now the North Mall. The abbey was founded in 1229 by the Irish chieftain, Dermot McCarthy, King of Desmond who was loyal to the English monarch at the time, Henry II. It became commonly known as the North Abbey and flourished for nearly three centuries in particular in terms of the size of its constant population and the financial support of the surrounding lay community in Munster. From the available Franciscan records, it is clear that provincial chapters or national gatherings of the Franciscan monks also took place at the abbey. The years included 1244, 1288, 1291, 1521 and 1533. Indeed, the first Franciscan provincial chapter in Ireland was held at the North Abbey in 1244.

Perhaps the best-known remaining feature of the North Abbey is its well. The well is situated at the foot of a rock face, on the grounds of a new bar called the Abbey Tavern and is located within a stone-built well house. The entrance has a wooden panel with the date of 1688 in iron numbers on it. The well is said to be holy in nature but is not dedicated to any particular saint and at one time is reputed to have been used by Corkonians as a cure for sore eyes, consumption and other ailments.

Next to the well on its west side, there is a second stone walled room, which is partially cut out of the domineering rock face. The purpose of this room is unknown but the rockface forms the end wall a number of metres into this space. Legend has it that beyond this end wall is an underground passage leading up into the environs the Gurranabraher. However, the same legend does not relate any stories of its usage.

A Modest History

Folklore has it that the history of Christ Church extends back at least 1,000 years. The church presently standing is reputed to be the third on the site with the first one supposed to be Danish in origin and dating to around AD 1000. When the Anglo-Normans seized control of the Viking town of Cork in 1177, Christ Church was rebuilt as a stone structure on the same site as the first, in Anglo-Norman style.

The Anglo-Norman church was reputed to comprise a tower, a steeple and a belfry housing an unrecorded number of bells within thick walls. Within the church precinct was a college or a basic schoolhouse of unknown material, an almshouse, gardens, graveyard and houses for the priests. In the course of time, more features were added to the church complex, such as a crypt, a chapel in praise of the crusades in 1310, a hostel and an organ given by Sir Francis Drake, which he took from a Spanish galleon, around 1588.

The associated graveyard was the burial place of wealthy merchants and mayors of the walled town of Cork. One tomb still on display in Christ Church is the tomb of Thomas Ronan, Mayor of Cork in 1537 and 1549 and whose frontal stone slab depicts that of a skeleton with decaying flesh. The stone slab, now disfigured in parts, is called the 'Modest Man', and is situated in the west end of Christ Church.

Christ Church ceased to function as a place of worship in 1978 due to a dwindling congregation and the building was purchased by Cork City Council in 1979 for the sum of £20,000. The Cork Archives Institute resided in Christ Church from 1979 until its relocation to a new purpose-built building in Blackpool in 2005. In 2008 Cork City Council committed to a €4.8 million project to restore and develop the historically significant building and they were successful in obtaining €2.18 million of funding from EU Structural Funds 2007-2013, the European Regional Development Fund and the Southern and Eastern Regional Assembly. The refurbishment of Christ Church includes the integration of the Triskel Arts Centre building located next door on Tobin Street. The two buildings are joined to the church via an extensive glazed link creating a beautiful new venue within the city to house creative performances and visual art.

A Centre of Conservation

In 1608, according to the charter of English King James I, the walled town of Cork contained two parishes, one on the marshy island with South Main Street as the backbone, whilst North Main Street was the centre of another marshy island and the other parish. In each parish, a basic stone church existed. Adjacent to South Main Street was Christ Church and the other was St Peter, which overlooked North Main Street. Up to the time of the Reformation in the sixteenth century, these churches were Christian, but after King Henry VIII's reign became solely Protestant.

Today St Peter's church is the second church to be built on its present site overlooking North Main Street. The first church was built some time in the early fourteenth century. In 1782 that church was taken down and, in 1783, the present limestone church was begun. At a later stage, a new tower and spire were added to the basic rectangular plan. The new spire had to be taken down due to the marshy ground on which it was built.

In recent years and in accordance to the aims of the pilot project of the Cork Historic Centre Action and the finance and support of Cork Civic Trust, St Peter's church has been extensively renovated and opened as an exhibition centre. One of the most interesting monuments on display in the church is the Deane monument. This monument, dating to 1710, was dedicated to the memory of Sir Matthew Deane and his wife and both are depicted on the monument, shown in solemn prayer on both sides of an altar tomb.

The Bells of Shandon

The name Shandon comes from the Irish word *Sean Dún*, which means old fort and it said to mark the ring fort of the Irish family MacCarthaigh, who lived in the area around AD 1000. St Anne's church, Shandon was built in 1722. In 1750, the firm of Abel Rudhall in Gloucester cast the famous bells of Shandon. Inscriptions can be found on the bells, which contain messages of joy and death. The clock on Shandon is an efficient timekeeper, except for the fact that the minute hands on the east and west faces always go ahead of their accomplices, the north and south hands, in the ascent from the half hour to the hour. It therefore gained the nickname, 'the four-faced liar'. Nevertheless, complete concurrence is attained once more at the hour.

The peculiar feature of the tall church tower, approximately 40 metres in height, is that the north and east sides are comprised of red sandstone, while the south and west sides are composed of grey hewn limestone. Rising from the main tower, which is in the shape of a telescope, are three further tiers, which end in a curved dome. Above this is an ornamental gold-coloured gilt sphere, which is crowned by the cardinal points, north, south, west and east, and a weather vane in the form of a fish. The giant gilded fish, 4-5 metres in length, symbolises salmon fishing. The clock of Shandon, with its four white faces, was made by James Mangan, a successful Cork watchmaker, and installed by Cork Corporation in 1847.

The North Cathedral

The present Catholic Cathedral of St Mary's and St Anne's is the fifth church on the site since the early 1600s (earlier incarnations were built in 1624, 1700, 1730, and 1808). The story of the present-day structure is as follows. In 1820, an immense fire greatly damaged the fourth cathedral so much so that it was only really the skeleton structure of the burned cathedral that survived. However, all was not lost and shortly after, the Roman Catholic Bishop of that time, John Murphy, delegated to architect George Pain the rebuilding of the then twelve-year-old cathedral, inside and outside. George Pain was also responsible for the design of buildings such as Holy Trinity church, St Patrick's church and Blackrock Castle.

In 1868, at an influential meeting of Catholic citizens, convened by then Bishop of Cork and Cloyne, William Delany, more alterations and improvements to the church were debated. By the proposed plans, the church was to be enlarged to double its contemporary size and a magnificent spire added. The new church would comprise a nave, choir, a chancel with four chapels and transepts with side aisles. The project ran into financial difficulty and many of the proposals were never carried out. Instead of the proposed spire, four pinnacles were designed and constructed. At a height of 46m, the present-day cathedral stands 3m higher than the adjacent tower of St Anne's church, Shandon.

A Structure Worthy of its Name

St Fin Barre's Cathedral is a marker of the once-vibrant early Christian monastery (built around AD 600) of St Finbarre. The present cathedral is the fifth known church on the site. The small medieval one was taken down in 1735 and is reputed to be the church in which the famous poet Edmund Spenser married his second wife, Elizabeth Boyle, in 1592. The second, or eighteenth-century, church was consecrated in 1735. It was a plain Classical building, which retained the original tower of the first church. It was taken down in 1865 to make way for, in the words of the bishop of Cork, Gregg at the time, 'a structure more worthy of the name, Cork Cathedral'.

A competition was held and the unanimous choice out of sixty-eight entrants from Ireland, Britain and the Continent was Londoner William Burges for the design inscribed '*Non Mortuus*

St Fin Barre's Cathedral, 1884. (*Illustrated London News*)

Sed Virescrit', which means 'He is not dead but flourishing'. The large rose-type stained-glass windows provide a colourful array of light inside the church. The great piers, which support the roof, are of grey-brown Stourton stone. The reddish columns are of Cork red marble. Architect William Burges accumulated artists and craftsmen who under his direct control were responsible for stained glass, woodwork, mosaics and metalwork. The sanctuary of St Fin Barre's Cathedral explodes in many colours – green and red columns, gilded capitals, and a ceiling patterned in red, blue, gold, white and green. See inside the cathedral for more information and a guided tour.

The Byzantine Church

Between the years 1730 and 1750, evidence shows that the Franciscan Order was active in three main areas in the city: near Shandon, Cotner's Lane and on Duncombe's Marsh (near the Grand Parade today). By 1750, the Franciscans had moved from North Main Street and had by now set up a friary in Broad Lane which today is part of the present site of St Francis's church. It was here that they remained until the present day. In 1937, it was decided that a new modern church would have to be built. Rebuilding commenced after the Second World War. The new church was ceremonially blessed and opened four years later, on 14 July 1953, by the Most Revd Dr Cornelius Lucey. St Francis' church has a Byzantine style of architecture and its interior is richly decorated with mosaics. St Anthony's Shrine, situated within the church, is one of the best architectural designs in the city.

BELONGING TO THE PEOPLE

A Monument to Martyrs

The main entrance into the City Hall is through a marble paved vestibule illustrating the Cork coat of arms and showing sculptures of two famous lord mayors of Cork, Tomás Mac Curtain and Terence Mac Swiney. Both Lord Mayors were actively involved in the struggle for Irish War of Independence and both died in office as a result of their involvement.

Cork City Hall is the second structure of its kind to be built on its site. The first was originally a Corn Exchange in the 1800s. The corn industry in Cork was a major source of revenue for farmers at the time. In 1883, it was decided by a number of Cork businessmen that the Corn Exchange should be converted into an exhibition centre, which in the late 1800s became Cork's City Hall. In the early hours of Sunday morning on 12 December 1920, the nineteenth-century building was destroyed by fire by British ex-army soldiers, the Black and Tans.

Irish President Eamon De Valera officially opened the new City Hall on 8 September 1936. The building, built in Neo-Classical Doric style, is a fine structure comprised of limestone from Little Island Quarries in County Cork. The building holds the principal departments of Cork City Council, including the Lord Mayor's Office.

A Great Train Station

Kent Station was originally built to replace the Dublin and Cobh termini, which were situated at Penrose Quay and Summerhill respectively. In the early 1880s, it was proposed by the leading railway company in Cork City, the Great Southern and Western Railway, to construct Kent Station. By 1890, the marshy land at the back of the houses on the lower Glanmire Road, overlooking the River Lee, was filled in. In the spring of 1891, the real construction work began on the main building of the station. The contractor was Samuel Hill, who was a native of Cork City. The style of architecture chosen for the station was basic and plain, primarily comprising ruabon brick faced with limestone. Two years later, the station was completed and opened in February 1893, adjacent to the railway tunnel constructed under Blackpool.

Kent Station is dedicated to the memory of Thomas Kent who fought in the aftermath of the Easter Rising. He was executed by the British Government on 9 May 1916 and was buried at the then Victoria (Collins) detention barracks – now Cork Prison.

In the 1970s, the station was temporarily renamed 'Folkstone Harbour' and became the backdrop for a major part of the film *The Great Train Robbery*, starring Sean Connery and Lesley Anne Downes.

Coming and Going

Few among passengers or staff mourned the passing of the old Grand Parade bus depot, which even by 1939 had become too small and congested for the growing numbers of people travelling by bus. It had been opened at 40/41 Grand Parade by the Irish Omnibus Company as the terminus for county buses in Cork in 1927 but an internal report in July 1939 described 'scenes of congestion and chaos which would not be allowed in any civilised city' at the depot during peak travel periods. On Monday 16 October 1944, bus passengers said farewell to the depot and services moved to the building at the junction of Parnell Place and Anderson's Quay, which was itself replaced in 1960 by the present bus station.

From January 1945 the Great Southern Railways (GSR) became part of Córas Iompair Éireann (CIE) – the new national transport organisation formed by an amalgamation of the GSR with the Dublin United Transport Company. The familiar red-and-white colour scheme of the Cork buses gradually gave way to the dark green livery of the new company. This nostalgic loss was balanced somewhat by growth and expansion as the end of the Emergency period of the Second World War brought a restoration of services, the opening of new routes and the advent of new buses to replace those worn out by the abnormal operating conditions. Today Cork Bus Station is a listed building and recently underwent a revamp.

3

THE PEOPLE WHO SHAPED CORK

ARTISTS, ARCHITECTS AND SCULPTORS

Knowledge and Culture: James Barry, artist (1741-1806)
Cork-born James Barry first attempted oil painting at about the age of 17. By the time he first went to Dublin, at the age of 22, he had produced several large paintings. In particular, he produced the painting that first brought him into public notice and gained him the acquaintance and patronage of Edmund Burke. The picture depicted the legendary landing of St Patrick on the coast of Cashel and of the conversion and baptism of the king of that district by the patron saint of Ireland. It was exhibited in London in 1762. Through the auspices of Burke and his other friends, James was able to study and paint abroad in the latter part of 1765. He went first to Paris, then to Rome and then on to Florence, Bologna and Venice.

In 1774, a proposal was made through Valentine Green to James Barry and Sir Joshua Reynolds and other artists to decorate the Great Room of the Society for the Encouragement of Arts, Manufactures and Commerce (Royal Society of Arts), in London's Adelphi, with historical and allegorical paintings. In 1777, James Barry made an offer to paint the whole room on condition that he was allowed the choice of his subjects, and that he would be paid by the society the costs of canvas, paints and models. His offer was accepted. He finished the series of pictures after seven years to the satisfaction of the members of the society, who granted him two exhibitions and at subsequent periods voted him 250 guineas and a gold medal. The series of six paintings were known as *The Progress of Human Knowledge and Culture*. Soon after his return from the Continent, James Barry was chosen as a member of the Royal Academy.

On the Walls of Westminster: Daniel Maclise, artist (1806-1870)
As a young man, Daniel Maclise was eager for culture, fond of reading and anxious to become an artist. His father, however, placed him in Newenham's Bank in 1820, where he remained for two years and then left to study in the Cork School of Art. In 1825 it happened that Sir Walter Scott was travelling in Ireland and young Maclise, having seen him in a bookshop, made a

Daniel Maclise, 1868. (*Illustrated London News*)

sketch of the great man. It was exceedingly popular and the artist became celebrated enough to receive many commissions for portraits, which he executed, in careful detail in pencil.

In 1829, Daniel exhibited for the first time in the Royal Academy. Gradually he began to confine himself more exclusively to subject and historical pictures. In 1835 the *Chivalric Vow of the Ladies* and the *Peacock* procured his election as associate of the Academy, of which he became a full member in 1840. In 1858, Daniel Maclise commenced one of the two great monumental works of his life, *The Meeting of Wellington and Blücher*, on the walls of Westminster Palace. It was begun in fresco, a process, which proved unmanageable. Daniel wished to resign the task but was encouraged by Prince Albert to complete it. Daniel had studied the new method of water-glass painting in Berlin, and carried out the Westminster subject and its companion, *The Death of Nelson*, in that medium, completing the latter painting in 1864.

The Institutions of Benson: John Benson, architect (1812-1874)
John Benson was born in a one-storey thatched house in the village of Collooney, County Sligo, in 1812. At an early age he showed architectural ability and so Edmund Joshua Cooper, of Markree Castle, Collooney, sent him to a technical school in Dublin at the age of 21. That was the only architectural training that John Benson received. He first obtained a post with the Board of Works. Later he was appointed County Surveyor, first for the West Riding of Cork in 1846 and then, in the same year, for the East Riding. After that, he was appointed Surveyor of the County of the City of Cork in 1851 and Engineer for the Harbour and Port of Cork. He held the latter two posts until his retirement. In 1852, despite very extensive international competition, John Benson's design was accepted for the buildings to house the Dublin Exhibition of 1853. He supervised the construction himself, and at the opening of the exhibition he was knighted by the Lord Lieutenant of Ireland.

In 1855, John designed the Cork Athenaeum, which later became the much-loved Cork Opera House (in 1877). He also designed other Cork institutions, such as the triumphal entrance of Shandon Butter Market and the elaborate brickwork of the English Market entrance on Princes Street. In the 1860s, John designed the Berwick Fountain on the Grand Parade, the current St Patrick's Bridge and various churches in Cork such as the revamp of the North Cathedral.

Hogan's Genius: John Hogan, sculptor (1800-1858)

John Hogan was born in Tallow, County Waterford, on 14 October 1800 and spent his youth in Cork City. He took up carpentry at an early age. His talent for draughtsmanship and carving was recognised and he was encouraged to take up sculpture by the architect, Sir Thomas Deane. John Hogan went to Rome where he studied at the School of St Luke and the Vatican galleries and established a studio there. John Hogan's best-known works are the three versions of the statue of *The Redeemer in Death* or *The Dead Christ*. Created in flawless Carrara marble, the first version (1829) is located in St Therese's church, Clarendon Street, Dublin, the second (1833) in St Finbarr's (South) Church Cork and the third and final version (1854) is located in the Basilica of St John the Baptist, Newfoundland. John Hogan assured his international reputation in 1829 with *The Dead Christ*. Thereafter, Irish bishops visiting his Rome studio bought his creations. The Danish sculptor Bertel Thorwaldsen pronounced that John was 'the best sculptor I leave after me in Rome'.

Studies of People: Joseph Higgins, sculptor (1885-1925)

Joseph Higgins was born in Ballincollig, County Cork, in 1885 and moved to Cork City with his family when he was 14. Joseph went to work at Newsom's tea merchants, and enrolled as a night student at the Crawford School of Art. There he trained in Arts and Crafts, specialising in wood and stone-carving and clay modelling, winning many prizes during his time there. His first portrait head was of writer Daniel Corkery, who encouraged and supported him throughout his life.

In 1910, Joseph won the highest award of the Annual South Kensington Scheme for a study from life of a child in clay (*Boy with a Boat*). He also that year won several prizes for wood-carving at the Royal Dublin Society. Two years later his *Study of an Old Woman (Nana) and Liam* were the first of many sculptures (and paintings) that he exhibited at the Royal Hibernian Academy, then the most important annual exhibition in Ireland.

Joseph was appointed art teacher in East Cork in 1913. In 1915 he married fellow Crawford student Katherine Turnbull, and they moved to Youghal. In an active life of teaching (travelling between Youghal, Fermoy and Midleton), he produced portraits of his own family, of neighbours and of Youghal fishermen. Among his other clay models were Michael Collins and W.F. Stockley.

The Foremost Sculptor: Seamus Murphy, sculptor (1907-1975)
Born near Burnfort, County Cork, in 1907, Seamus Murphy was one of the foremost stone carvers and sculptors of his time. From 1922 until 1930 he worked as an apprentice stone carver at O'Connell's Art Marble Works in Blackpool, Cork. He received a scholarship in 1931, which enabled him to go to Paris where he was a student at Académie Colarossi and studied with the Irish-American sculptor, Andrew O'Connor. After returning to Ireland, Seamus worked in O'Connell's stone yard. In 1934, he opened his own studio at Blackpool. Among his first commissions were the Dripsey Ambush Memorial and the Clonmult memorial at Midleton, two statues for Bantry church and a carved figure of St Gobnait in Ballyvourney graveyard.

The Virgin of the Twilight was exhibited at the Royal Hibernian Academy in 1944, and was later erected at Fitzgerald's Park, Cork. In 1939 he exhibited at the World Fair, New York. In 1944 he was elected as an Associate of Royal Hebernian Society (RHA). That same year he married Maighread Higgins, daughter of Cork sculptor Joseph Higgins. In 1945 Seamus designed Blackpool church for William Dwyer and in 1948 he carved the apostles and St Brigid for a church in San Francisco. Another of his sculptures is in St Paul's, Minnesota. He was made a full member of the RHA in 1954. He became professor of sculpture at the RHA in 1964, and was awarded an Hon. LLD by the National University of Ireland in 1969.

BUSINESS PEOPLE

Across the Atlantic: James Beale, shipbuilder (1798-1879)
James set up a business on Penrose Quay as a shipbuilder. His company, the St George Steam Packet Company, commissioned

the *Sirius*, the first steamship to make the trans-Atlantic crossing in 1838 from Cork to New York (31 March to 22 April). James worked for a time as a partner with his brother-in-law, Robert John Lecky, running a ship-repair yard at Penrose Quay. He was an enthusiastic watercolour painter and travelled extensively in Italy, Norway and Morocco. His paintings comprise *A Storm off the Bay of Tangiers* and *Skelligs Night on the South Mall*.

Arnott's Ambitions: Sir John Arnott, entrepreneur (1814-1898)
John was born in 1814 in Auchtermuchty, Scotland but his family moved to Cork during his youth. In 1837, he opened a small drapery business on St Patrick's Street. The business failed and John relocated to Belfast where he became very successful. He returned to Cork in the late 1840s and second time round became well established in drapery manufacture. He served for three years as Mayor of Cork (1859-1861) and was knighted by the Lord Lieutenant in November 1859 on the occasion of the laying of the foundation stone of the new St Patrick's Bridge in Cork City. John was elected as Liberal MP for Kinsale in 1859 and served until 1863. He was the founder of the Arnott's chain of stores, the owner of Arnott's Brewery and a chain of bakeries. In 1873, he purchased *The Irish Times* and, from 1872 until 1897, he was the owner of the Passage and Rushbrooke Docks. He was also a noted philanthropist and gave multiple donations to charity during his lifetime.

Musgrave's Delights: Stuart and Thomas Musgrave, grocers
In 1876 the brothers Stuart and Thomas Musgrave opened a grocery shop on North Main Street in Cork. They were aged 25 and 18 and had moved to Cork from County Leitrim. The business incorporated in 1894 as Musgrave Brothers Ltd, with a charter to retail and wholesale sugar, coffee, tea, spices, fruit, olive oil, and other foodstuffs. The company also ran a bakery and confectionary and was listed as a mineral water manufacturer, iron and hardware merchant, druggist, fish and ice merchant, stationer and haberdasher.

At the same time, the Musgrave Brothers built and ran Cork's iconic Metropole Hotel, as well as a sweet factory and a laundry. The first Musgrave grocery shop relocated to larger premises at

84 Grand Parade and by 1896 the brothers had opened a grocery shop in Tralee, County Kerry. In 1925 the company moved to a large new premises on Cornmarket Street. The extensive grocery warehouse gave the company significant competitive advantage over other wholesale grocers in the area. By this time the business was almost exclusively wholesale.

Today Musgrave serves more than 3,000 stores in Ireland, the UK and Spain and has annual wholesale turnover of €4.4 billion and global retail sales of €6.7 billion.

O'Sullivan's Tobacco Factory:
Patrick O'Sullivan, merchant (1885-1963)

Paddy O'Sullivan was one of nine brothers and two sisters who were born to a rural family in Clondrohid, near Macroom, County Cork. In 1905 he saw an abandoned store with a 'to let' sign in the window on Princes Street and established a wholesale base from which to work. Around 1910, Paddy's brother Michael left the drapery trade to form the partnership that is known as M.&P. O'Sullivan. Paddy O'Sullivan, keen to develop his business, diversified into tobacco manufacture. He proved himself to be a shrewd and astute entrepreneur, travelled to America to study the techniques of growing and processing tobacco. In 1927, Paddy O'Sullivan investigated the idea of establishing a tobacco factory in Cork and built a tobacco and snuff manufacturing plant in Mary Street. The company added wholesale grocery to its tobacco business in 1933 with a shop on Princes Street, Cork.

Today M.&P. O'Sullivan Ltd is still a successful, Irish-owned and entrepreneurial company.

Sunbeam's Ray of Hope:
William Dwyer, textiles manufacturer (1887-1951)

Born in Cork to a prominent business family, William was educated at Downside Abbey, England. In 1928, William established the Sunbeam Knitwear Company in Blackpool, Cork. The firm became known as Sunbeam Wolsey Ltd in 1933 when Wolsey, an English textile firm, was acquired. In the late 1940s, further factories were built at Youghal (Seafield Fabrics) and Midleton (worsteds and Woolcombers). By 1950, the combined workforce of the Dwyer firms numbered 2,000 people.

Dwyer unsuccessfully contested a Cork City seat for Fine Gael in the 1943 General Election, but standing as an independent candidate in 1944, he topped the poll. However, he resigned his seat in 1946. In 1948, he stood as an independent candidate for the East Cork constituency but failed to win a seat.

Throughout his life, William was a significant contributor to many charities. In 1945, he commissioned Seamus Murphy to design the Church of Annunciation in Blackpool, which he had built in memory of his daughter, Maeve, and which he presented to that Cathedral Parish.

JOURNALISTS AND WRITERS

Intellectual Ballads: Denny Lane, writer (1818-1895)

Denny Lane was the only child of Maurice Lane and Ellen Madden. His father was proprietor of the Glynntown Distillery in Riverstown, near Glanmire, County Cork. He was educated in Cork and at the age of 17 received a scholarship to study at Trinity College Dublin where he obtained a Master of Arts

Denny Lane. (Cork City and County Archives)

Degree, continuing his studies to become a barrister. On the death of his father in 1845, Denny finished his career as a barrister, returning to Cork where he took up the family business. Succeeding his father, he was instrumental in persuading the other Cork distillers to amalgamate and establish the Cork Distilleries Company. Very active in the business life of the city, Denny became the first Secretary and then Resident Engineer of the Cork Gas Company, a director of Belvelly Brickworks and Springfields Starch Works, Chairman of

Macroom Railway Co. and a director of the Cork, Blackrock and Passage Railway Company.

Denny Lane had an acute interest in the arts and in promoting and studying Irish music and culture. He was very active in the Schools of Art, Music and Design. He was a founder member and Vice-President of the Cork Historical and Archaeological Society and Chairman of the School of Science. He wrote many songs, the best remembered being the ballads, *Rose of Araglen* and *Carrigdhoun*.

The Cork Examiner *is Born:*
John Francis Maguire, politician and writer (1815-1872)
John Maguire founded the *Cork Examiner* in 1841 in support

John Francis Maguire by artist Daniel Maclise.

of Daniel O'Connell. He was called to the Bar in 1843 and was a Member of Parliament for Dungannon from 1852 to 1865. In 1865, he became MP for Cork, supporting nationalist policies on the land question, disestablishment and reform of the Poor Law while he was in parliament. He was also Lord Mayor of Cork four times. He made three visits to Pope Pius IX in Rome and published a book on the pontificate which prompted the pope to name him Knight Commander of St Gregory. He published at least another five books, among them *The Irish In America*, which was written after a six-month trip to America and Canada in the 1850s.

An Evening Echo: Thomas Crosbie, journalist (1827-1899)
Thomas was born in Arfert, County Kerry in 1827. He was educated locally and at the age of 15, joined the reporting staff of the *Cork Examiner*, which had been founded the previous year by John Francis Maguire. Thomas later became Maguire's partner and effectively the managing director of the newspaper. On Maguire's death, he bought out the proprietorship. Under his management, the *Cork Examiner*, which had been published three times a week, became a daily. The *Evening Echo* was launched in 1892 and a weekly edition, the *Cork Weekly Examiner* appeared in 1895. Crosbie served as President of both the Irish Association of Journalists and of the Institute of Journalists.

A Hidden Ireland: Daniel Corkery, writer (1878-1964)
Daniel commenced his writing at the turn of the twentieth century in the columns of D.P. Moran's brashly polemical nationalist weekly the *Leader*. He developed into a sensitive short-story writer, but also included a well-regarded novel, *The Threshold of Quiet* (1917), among his prose publications. He is best remembered, however, as a propagandist for the ideas of the Irish Ireland movement, and his two critical studies, where he discussed these ideas at length, have been the subject of much controversy. *The Hidden Ireland* (1924) is a study of the eighteenth-century literary remnants of an Irish-language literary culture stretching back almost 2,000 years. In it Corkery attempts to reconstruct the Gaelic world view which, he argues, was preserved in reduced circumstances by the poets amongst the impoverished, oppressed Catholic peasantry of the Penal Law era. A prominent classic, its

version of the past offered powerful cultural support to the traditional nationalist history that was emerging in the Irish Free State.

The Nest of a Great Writer: Seán O'Faoláin, writer (1900-1991)

One of Ireland's great writers, Corkman Seán O'Faoláin was born in the heart of the city, the son of an RIC constable. As a young man, O'Faoláin became committed to the cause of the IRA. He served as a bomb-maker and then as director of publicity. After the War of Independence, he took up a fellowship at Harvard. In 1932, he founded the Irish Academy of Letters, along with G.B. Shaw, W.B. Yeats, Frank O'Connor and a number of other important literary figures.

Sean O'Faoláin's first novel, *A Nest of Simple Folk*, was published in 1933 to great critical acclaim. However, it was to be his short story writing that made him widely known. In his career, he penned four novels and numerous shorts stories. He also wrote a number of biographies, including his own entitled *Vive Moi!* in 1965. He penned several travel books and works of literary criticism. During the first half of the 1940s, he edited the distinguished literary magazine, *The Bell*. Unfortunately, throughout his career much of his work was censored, but in 1989, two years before his death, he became a freeman of Cork.

A Master of the Short Story: Frank O'Connor, writer (1903-1966)

Frank O'Connor, the pseudonym of Michael Francis O'Donovan, was born in Cork on 17 September 1903. He was born on Douglas Street but shortly afterwards moved to 251 Blarney Street where his early childhood was spent playing under the watchful Shandon tower. At five years old, he and his family moved to Harrington Square in the Dillon's Cross district. While a child, O'Connor came under the tutorage of Daniel Corkery, who developed and nurtured his love of Gaelic literature, Irish drama and the artistic heritage of Europe. With this love, O'Connor fought in the Irish Civil War in the early 1920s and was interned in Gormanstown Camp, County Meath for his Republican activities.

After his release, Frank O'Connor worked as a librarian in Sligo and Wicklow. In 1925 he became Librarian of Cork County. In 1938, he resigned from the Cork post and decided to devote himself to literature. He thereafter made his living through writing, lecturing and broadcasting. He spent much time in England and the USA. O'Connor's work included two novels, a biography of Michael Collins, *The Big Fellow* (1937), and translations from the Irish literary criticisms and dramatisations. His first volume of short stories was *Guests of the Nation* (1930), which drew on material from his experiences while running dispatches during the War of Independence. Other collections were *Bones of Contention* (1936), *Crab Apple Jelly* (1944), *Traveller's Samples* (1951) and *Domestic Relations* (1957). He also wrote two volumes of auto-biography, *A Lonely Child* (1961) and *My Father's Son* (1969). His critical work included *The Lonely Voice, A Study of the Short Story* (1962). Throughout his work, O'Connor recorded what he deemed the 'flashpoints' of human existence.

Frank O'Connor died in Dublin of a heart attack on 10 March 1966.

Poetic Etchings: Seán Ó Riordáin, writer (1916-1977)

Seán was born in Ballyvourney but the family moved to Inniscarra in 1932, following the death of his father. He attended North Monastery CBS, Cork. In 1937, he took a job as a clerk with Cork Corporation, but a year later, tuberculosis was diagnosed and eventually he was hospitalised at Doneraile where he wrote his first poem. His poetic collections include *Eireabll Spideóige* (1952), *Brosna* (1964), *Línte Líombó* (1971) and *Tar éis mo Bháis* (1979). In 1965, he resigned from Cork Corporation through ill health. In 1967, with Seamus Ó Chonghaile, he published *Rí na hUile*. He worked as a part-time lecturer at University College Cork from 1969. The National University of Ireland conferred him with an honorary D.Litt in 1976.

MUSICIANS

Our Musical Heritage: Seán O'Riada, composer (1931-1971)

Seán O'Riada was born in Cork in August 1931. He grew up and was educated in County Limerick but returned to UCC as a student in 1948 and studied his great passions, classics and music. He was employed by Radió Éireann as assistant music director, but left in 1956 to explore other musical cultures, eventually studying piano in Paris. He later penned national radio broadcasts entitled 'Our Musical Heritage'. In 1959, O'Riada produced his most well-known work, *Mise Eire*, a short film about Ireland's struggle for freedom. His interpretation of Irish music proved his genius. He revitalised the traditional music scene, enriched the sound of traditional music and brought it to greater audiences. During the 1960s, his career went from strength to strength, creating scores for *Saorse*, *The Playboy of the Western World* and *Young Cassidy*. His formation of the popular group Ceoltoirí Chulann brought a fresh approach to Irish music. In 1963, O'Riada was appointed lecturer at University College Cork. In 1968, his accomplishments were celebrated when he received the Irish Composer of the Year award in Belfast. O'Riada died in October 1971.

German Music Connections:
Aloys Fleischmann, composer (1912-1992)
Of German origin, Aloys was at the centre of music in Cork for over fifty years, especially in the latter half of the twentieth century. He was professor of music in University College Cork, a conductor, scholar, teacher and composer who devoted his life and energies to the development of music and art in the city of Cork. He campaigned for Cork Corporation to put music on the school curriculum and subsequently a School of Music was built. Fleishman established the Cork Orchestral Society, which gave amateur musicians an opportunity to perform the great works to an appreciative audience. Fleischmann also directed and organised the Cork International Choral Festival, an event that gave local choirs, in particular in rural areas, a forum to compete against other choirs from home and abroad. Aloys Fleischmann was conferred the freedom of the city in 1978.

Cork's Ballet Group: Joan Denise Moriarty, dancer (1912-1992)
At a young age Joan Denise Moriarty developed a love of dance, especially ballet. She trained in London and Paris to become a professional dancer, but due to illness she could not fulfil her dream. In 1941, she returned to Cork where she opened her own dance school in St Patrick's Street and formed the Cork Ballet Group, later the Cork Ballet Company. In 1959, Joan established the Irish Theatre Ballet, which went on tour nationally, but

after five years financial problems forced it to close. However, shortly afterwards the Irish Government gave Moriarty funds to establish the Irish National Ballet.

Singing the Blues: Rory Gallagher, musician (1948-1995)
Rory although born in Ballyshannon in County Donegal, grew up and was educated in the heart of Cork City. He pursued his passion for music as soon as he heard the sound of Chuck Berry, Little Richard, Carl Perkins, Lonnie Donegan and Elvis Presley on the radio, and later listening to American Forces Network where he heard Woody Guthrie, Leadbelly and Muddy Waters. He was a self-taught musician and mastered the acoustic guitar in his early teens, progressing to his renowned (1961) Fender Stratocaster Guitar – a Sunburst Model purchased (second hand) at the age of 15 from Crowleys Music Store in Cork in 1963 for £100. He acknowledged throughout his career the major influence that the music of African American musicians such as Muddy Waters, Howlin' Wolf, Buddy Guy, Big Bill Broonzy, Blind Boy Fuller, Son House and Tampa Red had on his repertoire.

During his career Rory sold over 30 million albums worldwide and had a major following in Germany, Austria, Switzerland and Holland. The interest in his output has grown since his untimely death in June 1995 with tribute shows in Spain, USA, Sweden, Scotland, Holland, Wiesbaden in Germany, Cork and the Annual Tribute Festival in Ballyshannon, County Donegal. He died suddenly on 14 June 1995.

REVOLUTIONARIES

Washington's General: Stephen Moylan (1737-1811)
Stephen Moylan was a Catholic who was educated in Paris. He entered the shipping business, first in Lisbon and then in Philadelphia, where he moved in 1768. The Corkman joined the American Continental Army and George Washington appointed him Muster-Master General in August 1775. On 7 June 1776, Congress appointed him Quartermaster General to succeed Thomas Mifflin. Late in 1776, upon orders from Washington, Stephen organised and took command of a

regiment of dragoons, which became a part of the American cavalry commanded by General Pulaski. His military career ended after the surrender of Cornwallis at Yorktown, when ill health forced him to return to his home in Philadelphia. Stephen spent the greater portion of his life in Philadelphia, but for a while lived on a farm in Chester County, Pennsylvania. George Washington appointed Stephen Commissioner of Loans in Philadelphia – a position he occupied until his death on 13 April 1811, at the age of 74. He is buried in the grounds of St Mary's Catholic church in Philadelphia.

Bolivar's Aide-de-Camp:
Daniel Florence O'Leary, Venezuelan General (c.1802-1854)
Daniel was born at 89/90 Barrack Street, Cork, the son of Jeremiah O'Leary, a butter merchant. Unlike many of the Irish who fought for Bolívar in the South American wars of independence, Daniel had not served in the Napoleonic Wars. In 1817, he enlisted in Britain as a mercenary in the forces of Simon Bolívar the future liberator of Venezuela. In March 1820, Daniel was appointed aide-de-camp under Bolívar. Daniel later became a Lieutenant-Colonel and took part in many campaigns. After Bolívar's death, Daniel moved in turn to Jamaica and Venezuela and represented the Venezuelan Foreign Service in various European cities. In January 1841 he began working for the British Foreign Office, holding various consular positions. Daniel spent much of his later years writing his memories (spanning thirty-four volumes) of his time fighting in the wars of revolution with Simon Bolívar.

Fenian Presences: Brian Dillon, Fenian (1830-1872)
Brian Dillon was born at Banduff on Rathcooney Road, Cork. The family had a public house at the crossroads now known as Dillon's Cross. Brian received his education at city schools including the Cork School of Art. He then went to work as a clerk in the South Mall law office of W.P. Coppinger, solicitor, and soon became involved in the nationalist organisations, including the Fenian movement of which he became a local leader.

In 1865, he was arrested, charged with conspiracy and was sentenced to ten years' penal servitude. He served five years in Pentonville Gaol and later at Woking Gaol where his health deteriorated and where he was released on compassionate grounds. His return to Cork was marked by a large demonstration of support. He is buried under an elaborate high cross in Rathcooney Graveyard, Mayfield, Cork.

Murder in Blackpool:
Tomás MacCurtain, Lord Mayor (1884-1920)

Tomás MacCurtain was born in Ballyknockane, Mallow, County Cork. His passion for Irish culture led him to join the Cork-Blackpool branch of the Gaelic League in 1901. In 1907, MacCurtain contributed to the National Council of Sinn Féin and in the same year he became a member of the Irish Republican Brotherhood. He enlisted as an Irish Volunteer in late 1913 and was periodically imprisoned in various English jails, such as Reading, Wakefield and Frongoch. In early 1920 he was elected as a Sinn Féin Councillor for the electoral area of Cork North West, and on 20 January 1920, he became Lord Mayor of Cork. He was made commander of the IRA Cork Brigade. Early on the morning of 20 March 1920, Lord Mayor Tomás MacCurtain was found murdered at his home.

Victim of a Hunger Strike:
Terence MacSwiney, Lord Mayor (1879-1920)

Terence MacSwiney also took an active part in the Irish Volunteers and devoted much time to literary and dramatic groups such as the Young Ireland Society and the Celtic Literary Society. Between 1910 and 1914, MacSwiney wrote five plays, two of which were in verse. One of his greatest works, *The Principles of Freedom*, appeared in serial form in a Dublin monthly paper, *Irish Freedom*. After MacCurtain's murder, MacSwiney became his successor and claimed that the murder had been carried out by the Royal Irish Constabulary under the direction of the British Government. There was huge public outcry. MacSwiney was re-arrested and was transported to Brixton Prison where he died on 25 October 1920, after a hunger strike lasting seventy-four days.

SOCIAL ACTIVISTS

Nano's School for the Poor:
Nano Nagle, Presentation Sisters (1718-1784)
In the late 1750s, one of Cork's most famous historical characters, Nano Nagle made her first appearance as a strong force in quelling the terrible poverty in the city. Nano Nagle was born in Ballygriffin townland, near Mallow in north Cork in 1718. She was the eldest of seven children of wealthy, well-connected parents. At ten years of age, she left Ireland to attend school in Paris with her sister Anne. Nano remained in Paris after her schooling but was brought back to Ireland when her

Nano Nagle from William Hutch's *Nano Nagle* (Dublin, 1875).

father died. Her mother died in 1748 and Anne died a year later. Grief-stricken, she returned to Paris where she entered a convent and after several years of training, she again returned to Cork in 1754 to help the plight of the poor children in the city. Amidst the backdrop of influential charity schools in the city for Protestants, she particularly wished to provide education and instruction in the Catholic faith. Her first school was in a little rented cabin on Cobh Street, now Douglas Street and she provided food and medicine for the needy as well. Such was Nano Nagle's presence in the city that she established her own congregation of Presentation Sisters in 1776 known as the Sisters of the Charitable Instruction of the Sacred Heart of Jesus. Nano Nagle died on 26 April 1784, aged 65 years.

The Sisters of Charity:
Mary Aikenhead, Sisters of Charity (1787-1858)

Born on 19 January 1787 in Daunt's Square on the Grand Parade, Cork, Mary Aikenhead was baptised on 4 April into the Anglican community at St Anne's church, Shandon. In 1812, Mary Aikenhead departed the city for the Bar Convent in York in 1812. There, she met with Alicia Walsh. Both trained as novices following the Rule of Ignatius. Arriving back in Dublin in 1815, Mary and Alicia moved into a building in North William Street, off Summerhill, acquired by the newly elevated Archbishop Murray. Mary was given the religious name, Sr Mary Augustine and Alicia, the name of Sr Mary Catherine.

Mary and Catherine left the confines of the convent and began to visit the sick poor in their own homes. As the good reputation of the sisters spread, other women expressed an interest in joining the order. The number of sisters entering the order to minister to the poor rose steadily in Dublin, and soon further afield in cities such as Cork.

Mother Mary Aikenhead died in Harold's Cross in Dublin on 22 July 1858 and was buried in St Mary Magdalen's Cemetery, Donnybrook in Dublin. Her spiritual legacy provided the impetus for future Sisters of Charity to establish a large series of successful convents, schools and hospitals across the world.

Lecturing the Elite:
Thomas Dix Hincks, educationalist (1767-1857)

In 1790, Revd Thomas Dix Hincks arrived in Cork to take up his ministry at the principal Presbyterian Chapel on Princes Street. Born in Dublin in 1767, Thomas was the son of a customs official and was initially educated at Chester, England. He spent a short time at Trinity College before making it his intention to enter the Church of Ireland ministry, studying at Hackney under Joseph Priestley. At the age of 23, Thomas opened a private fee-paying school or academy at his house on St Patrick's Hill, where he taught classics as well as introducing a broader range of subjects in mathematics and elementary science.

By the closing years of the eighteenth century, Revd Thomas Dix Hincks had published a number of pamphlets, that addressed religious, social and educational issues on a European, national and local scale. In 1802, his main priority was education of the populace. The following year, the first course of free educational lectures for the general public was given by him in Cork. His institution was known as the Cork Institution, which received a royal charter in 1807. The institution was the forerunner of University College Cork and subsequently Cork Institute of Technology.

Taking the Temperance Pledge:
Fr Theobald Mathew, Temperance Movement (1790-1856)

Fr Mathew, a Tipperary man, was ordained a priest in the Capuchin order in 1814. Subsequently, he was assigned to the South Friary (now the site of the city's tax office) in Blackamoor Lane near Sullivans's Quay. Fr Mathew set up a girl's school with local Catholic ladies acting as governesses. He later established a boy's school near Blackamoor Lane. He involved many young people in his works of charity and founded the Josephine Society, a voluntary organisation whose members visited the sick and formed benefit societies for the unemployed. By the mid-1830s, the energy and forcefulness of Fr Mathew's work had marked him out as a visionary socialist.

Fr Mathew's most well-known contribution to society was the creation of an effective temperance movement. Among the many social problems afflicting the people of the country in the first half of the 1800s, drunkenness was a serious issue. Cheap to purchase,

Fr Theobald Mathew,
1843. (*Illustrated
London News*)

whiskey was the common choice across the classes. It was produced
in eighty distilleries, scattered fairly evenly among the larger towns.
There were also 240 breweries. In Cork, the largest brewery was
Beamish and Crawford, established in 1791. Also plying their
trade across the country were 400 spirit-dealers and about 20,000
licensed premises. In the 1830s, there were around 150 spirit-
dealers in Cork alone, not to mention the illegal traders of spirits.

By the end of 1840, 180,000 to 200,000 nationwide had taken
a pledge to stop drinking alcohol and Fr Mathew was acclaimed
as the 'Apostle of Temperance'. The effects were felt quickly: in
the early 1840s there were reports of better conduct, a decrease
in social order offences and the completion of proper work.
However, the alcohol industry did suffer. Consumption of legally
distilled spirits in Cork was almost halved. Many employed in
the production and sale of alcohol lost their jobs. However, none
of the breweries were forced to close.

Fr Mathew died of paralysis at Queenstown (now Cobh) in
December 1856. His remains were buried in his own cemetery in

Cork, St Joseph's cemetery, which he had created for the poor. He is remembered in Cork through events like Feis Matiú, which takes place in Fr Mathew Hall on Fr Mathew Street. William O' Connor, a merchant tailor in the city and a contemporary admirer of Fr Matthew, erected the Fr Mathew Tower at Dunsland, Glanmire in 1843. The most well-known commemorative feature in the city is the statue of Fr Mathew erected in 1864 on St Patrick's Street.

For the Love of Shakespeare:
Fr Christy O'Flynn, speech and drama teacher (1881-1961)
The Cork Shakespearean Society, known locally as 'The Loft', was established in 1924 by Father James Christopher O'Flynn. It was located on the floor above Linehan's sweet shop in John Redmond Street until 2000, when the Shakespearean Society moved to the nearby Firkin Crane premises. It subsequently moved to its current location in the basement of the North Cathedral Presbytery. Some of Ireland's best known performers, such as Joe Lynch, Niall Tóibín, and broadcaster Liam Ó Murchú performed there. The society has staged Shakespearean plays in theatres and halls around Cork since 1927. In 2014 it celebrated its 90th anniversary.

Science Lessons for the City:
Br James Burke, educationalist (1833-1904)
Br Burke was born in Limerick. He entered the novitiate of the Christian Brothers at Mount Sion, Waterford, in June 1852 and three months later was transferred to North Monastery CBS Cork City. There he continued his training and began his teaching career. He was a pioneer in Irish scientific and technical education. His colleagues were Br Michael Augustine O'Riordan, architect and John Holland, the inventor of the modern submarine. In 1869, with the financial help of Denny Lane, Martin F. Mahony, Joseph Ronayne and Richard Caulfield, he opened a science hall at North Monastery, which, by 1875 included an experimental department in physics and chemistry operated by the pupils. In 1876, he began work on his industrial and art museum, which in time, grew into a huge selection of curios. Two years later, he became superior of North Monastery School. In 1897, he initiated the building of Gerald Griffin

Memorial Technical School, where hundreds of Cork's craftsmen and tradesmen were trained.

A City's Technical Institute:
A.F. Crawford Sharman, philanthropist (1862-1943)

Born at Crawfordsburn in County Down in 1862, Arthur Frederick was the son of Arthur Johnson Sharman Crawford, barrister and company director. Arthur F. was a director of Beamish and Crawford Ltd. A generous benefactor, he provided the site for the building of the Sharman Crawford Municipal Technical Institute. When the site came into the possession of the Technical Instruction Committee it was a dreary waste of semi-ruinous buildings, but on making the plans for the new institute, it was found possible to incorporate some of the existing structures. They were made into laboratories, and the remainder of the old buildings, on being taken down, became a veritable mine for building materials. Arthur also provided the scholarships and financial support to the Cork School of Art. He was also a governor of the Cork Dairy Institute and a founder member of Cork Golf Club.

Seaside Excursions for the Poor:
Augustine Roche, Lord Mayor of Cork (1849-1915)

Augustine Roche was born at Douglas Street, where his father operated a wine business for many years. After his education was completed, Augustine entered the family business and expanded it throughout the county. He was an active supporter of the Land League in the 1880s. In 1883, he entered Cork Corporation and showed great interest in providing new houses and education for the working classes. In 1893, he was elected Mayor of Cork and was re-elected the following year. By that time, he was closely connected to several charitable institutions in the city and highlighted the plight of the city's more impoverished citizens. It was during his term of office that the excursion to the seaside for the poor children for one day a year was initiated. Augustine Roche was a prominent helper at the excursions. He also provided a Christmas dinner for the street traders who principally sold newspapers. He was returned as a Member of Parliament for the city in 1905 and represented the city until 1910.

CHARACTERS

Mayors and a Sugar Plantation:
Edward Galwey, sugar plantation owner (b. late seventeenth century)
The Galweys (variously spelled as Galway, Gallway, Gallaway and even Galvy) were an Anglo-Norman family, who became one of the dominant families in civic life in Cork City during the fifteenth and sixteenth century. The family were notably associated with Cork, Youghal and Kinsale. They provided thirty-nine mayors and forty-nine sheriffs of Cork City between 1422 and 1644. Through the English plantation period in the late sixteenth century, the Galweys lost much of their property in the city. Some of the exiled members settled in Nantes, France, where they ranked among the nobility. The Galweys were one of the principal Catholic families to settle extensively in the West Indies during the colonial period. In the late 1600s, David Galwey established a sugar plantation on the British Island colony of Monserrat in the West Indies.

Decoding Hieroglyphics:
Edward Hincks, antiquarian (1792-1866)
Edward Hincks was born in Cork and educated at Trinity College, Dublin. He took orders in the Church of Ireland and was rector of Killyleagh, County Down. From 1825 onwards, Edward Hincks devoted his spare time to the study of hieroglyphics and to the deciphering of cuneiform scripts. He became a pioneer, working out contemporaneously with Sir H. Rawlinson, and independently of him, the ancient Persian vowel system. He published a number of original and scholarly papers on Assyriological questions of the highest value, chiefly in the *Transactions of the Royal Irish Academy*. To celebrate his work, a bust of Edward Hincks is on display in the gardens of the Cairo Museum, Egypt.

A Canadian Prime Minister:
Francis Hincks, Premier of Canada (1807-1885)
Born in Cork, the son of a Thomas Dix Hincks, a Presbyterian minister, Francis Hincks went to York (Toronto) in 1832 and set up an importing business there. He accepted a job as manager

for the Farmer's Bank but became manager of the newly formed Bank of the People. He established *The Examiner* in Toronto, with the aim of promoting responsible government. He was elected to the First Parliament of United Canada in 1841, representing Oxford County. In 1842, Hincks was appointed Inspector General of Public Accounts. In 1844, he became editor of a new newspaper in Montreal, *The Pilot*, which supported political reformers in both Canada East and Canada West.

Francis Hincks was Premier of the Province of Canada from 1851 to 1854. Hincks' vision of a railroad linking British North America led to the establishment of the Grand Trunk in 1852 and he helped to negotiate the Reciprocity Treaty of 1854 with the United States. In 1856, he accepted an appointment as Governor of Barbados and the Windward Islands and in 1861, he became governor of British Guiana. He was knighted in 1869. On his return to Canada, he was Minister of Finance from 1869 until 1874. In 1878, he represented the federal government on the Ontario-Manitoba boundary commission. Francis was also an editor of the *Toronto Express* newspaper.

The Future of Ireland's Past:
Robert Day, antiquarian (1836-1914)

Robert Day (1836-1914) was an Irish antiquarian and photographer. He was involved in his family's extensive saddlery business, together with a sports shop well known to Cork anglers. His wife Rebecca belonged to the Scott family who had an extensive ironmongery business in King Street (now McCurtain Street). Robert was president of the Cork Cuverian Society and its successor, the Cork Historical and Archaeological Society, from 1894 to 1914. There, he gathered an enormous collection of Irish Archaeological artefacts, which were auctioned in 1915. An on-going project at the Archaeology Department of University College Cork is seeking to trace items from this auction. Some items are in the Hunt Museum in Limerick.

Robert's early photographs date from the 1860s. The pictures are now part of the Day collection, which also has photographs by his son William ('Willy') Tottenham Day (1874-1965) and grandson Alec (1902-1980). Another grandson was the noted writer and lithographer Robert Gibbings.

Botanic Interests
James Drummond, botanist (1787-1863)

James Drummond was born in Inverarity, Scotland and was an avid botanist and plant collector. From 1808 until 1829, he was curator at the Cork Botanical Gardens, which were under the aegis of the Royal Cork Institution. He was an associate of the Linnaean Society and published several papers on Irish plants. In 1829, James, together with his wife and six children, accompanied Captain Stirling to Western Australia on the ship *Parmelia*. James Drummond was appointed Government Naturalist but worked more in the role of botanist. He was also appointed superintendent of the Government Gardens and received a salary of £100. He went on numerous expeditions across Western Australia where he collected thousands of seeds and plants for export to England. Today his plant specimens are found in herbaria across the world. He named several of Western Australia's native species and 119 specimens have been names after him. Together with his sons, especially Johnston, and other botanists (including John Gilbert) he collected over 3,500 specimens.

The walled garden of the Cork Botanical Gardens can still be viewed in what is now St Joseph's Cemetery.

The Black Eagle of the North:
Fr John Murphy, explorer (1796-1883)

Born on 23 December 1796, John James Murphy was the second son of James Murphy, of Ringmahon, Cork. In fact, he was to become the uncle of James J. Murphy, who founded Murphy's brewery in 1854. John's youth was spent as a midshipman, a traveller in China and a financier in London. In North America his work with the Hudson Bay Company brought him close to the Indians who made him an Indian Chief and named him 'Black Eagle of the North'. During a severe illness he reputedly had a vision and as a result, went to the Beda College in Rome to study for the priesthood. Back in his native Cork City, Fr John Murphy commissioned the fashionable architect Edwin Pugin, with generous contributions from Murphy's distilleries, to design the church of St Peter and St Paul of which he was made an archdeacon.

The Real Taoiseach:
Jack Lynch, sportsman and Taoiseach (1917-1999)

Jack Lynch was a gifted sportsman. In the 1940s he played on the Cork All-Ireland minor and senior football teams, winning several All-Ireland medals. His second passion was politics, and he stood for Fianna Fail in the 1946 by-election, going on to serve as minister in the departments of Education and Industry and Commerce. In 1966, he succeeded Sean Lemass to become Taoiseach.

Crubeens on the Coal Quay:
Kathy Barry, publican (1909-1982)

Kathy ran a small provisions shop (now demolished) in Dalton's Avenue, off the Coal Quay. She was synonymous with the Coal Quay and famous for her crubeens, which were always in great demand once the local pubs had closed. There was also a chance of a few glasses for special customers. She lived in later years across the road at No.6 Corporation Buildings. She died at the Mercy Hospital, Cork on 17 December 1982 and was buried in St Joseph's Cemetery, Cork.

Design and Build:
John Sisk, contractor (1837-?)

John Sisk & Son Ltd – the company's name immediately tells us that it started as a small family business. The first John Sisk founded the business in Cork City in 1859 and the second John Sisk, the 'Son' in the name, took it forward to be a respected general contracting company operating in the province of Munster, building schools, churches, hospitals and public buildings. Yet it was the third John Sisk, who really grew it on a national and international scale. After graduating as a civil engineer, he joined his father on the building of the Cork City Hall in 1930 and moved to Dublin in 1937 to establish the company as a nationwide contractor. Hence the company secured many of the major public contacts of the period, including the iconic Industry and Commerce Building on Kildate Street, Dunlin and Ireland's first million-pound contract, a hospital for the treatment of tuberculosis, the first of three.

During the slump of the late 1950s, John G. Sisk established a branch in Africa, and the company later expanded rapidly when Ireland opened its doors to foreign investment in the 1960s and '70s. More recently, the company has become proficient at 'design and build' contracts, especially in the UK, where it has been operating successfully since the late 1980s. Similarly both civil engineering and residential construction are now major market sectors in which John Sisk & Son has a significant market share. The company is Ireland's largest and oldest construction company and one of Britain's top twenty such companies.

4

HIDDEN CORNERS

A CITY REMEMBERS

The Statue

Cork City has only one full-length statue on display in the public realm, that of Fr Theobald Mathew. Soon after the death of temperance campaigner Fr Mathew in December 1856, a committee was formed for the purpose of erecting a suitable memorial in the city. The commission was entrusted to the famous sculptor John Hogan who in his early days had been raised in Cove Street and was acquainted with Fr Mathew. Hogan died in 1858, before the statue was completed. On his death a meeting of the committee was called. It was reported that they had on hand the sum of £900, and on the motion of John Francis Maguire MP, it was agreed to give £100 to the Hogan family in recognition of what Hogan had already done on the contract. The sculptor's eldest son, John Valentine, endeavoured to carry out his father's work and in June 1858 another meeting of the community was held at the Athenaeum to inspect a model of a statue he brought to Cork.

However, the commission was handed over to John Henry Foley. He was the second son of Jesse Foley, a native of Winchester, who had settled in Dublin. When Foley had reached the age of 13 he decided to follow his eldest brother into the profession of sculptor. He entered the school of the Royal Dublin Society where he soon distinguished himself by winning many prizes for drawing and modelling. In 1823 he won the major award of that school. This success induced him to follow his brother to London where he joined the schools of the Royal Academy. Within a short time he submitted a study entitled 'The death of Abel', which won for him a ten-year scholarship to that establishment. Foley's next noteworthy achievement was exhibiting in the Royal Academy in 1839, and ten years later he was elected a full member, allowing him to add the letters 'RA' after his name. At 40 years of age the sculptor had achieved the highest honours.

Foley's output was prodigious and his works are to be found in India, USA, Sri Lanka, Ireland and Scotland. His subjects were deemed classical and imaginative, creating equestrian statues, monuments and portrait busts. Two years after the unveiling of the Fr Mathew statue, his Daniel O'Connell monument in Dublin was unveiled.

A National Monument

The National Monument on the Grand Parade honours the Irish patriots who fought in rebellions, including the United Irishmen who rose in 1798 under Wolfe Tone, the Young Ireland rebellion of 1848, and the Fenian Rising of 1867. An inscription on it reads:

> To perpetuate the Memory of the Gallant Men of 1798, 1803, 1848 and 1867 who fought and died in the wars of Ireland to recover her sovereign independence and to inspire the youth of our country to follow in their patriotic footsteps and imitate their heroic example. And righteous men will make our land A Nation Once Again.

Several lists of names are recorded on the monument, which features five statues: Mother Erin; Wolfe Tone, the leader of the 1798 rebellion; Fenian leader Peter O'Neill Crowley; Young Irelander Thomas Davis; and United Irishman leader Michael Dwyer. It was designed by well-known architect D.J. Coakley, and built by Ellis Coakley, who designed the façade of nearby Holy Trinity church. The neo-Gothic design of the monument bears a striking resemblance to the front of the church.

John Francis Davis, a Kilkenny man with a studio in Dublin, sculpted the statues. The Cork Young Ireland Society, a successor to the Cork '98 Centenary Committee, raised funds for its construction. Its foundation stone was laid in 1898, close to where a statue of George III on horseback once stood, but the finished structure was not unveiled until St Patrick's Day 1906. Unveiled by patriot Jeremiah O'Donovan Rossa, from Rosscarbery, County Cork, the landmark monument became a regular meeting place for many nationalist political meetings over the years.

First World War Memorial

At the South Mall is a memorial to those Irishmen who died in the First World War. It was erected in 1925, and is one of a few Irish examples. Carved in relief on a modest limestone obelisk, sitting on a plinth, is the profile of a Munster Fusiliers soldier in full military uniform, head down, gun at rest. Each November wreaths are laid here to mark the anniversary of the armistice of 1918. During the First World War over 2,000 Corkmen were killed, some 1,100 of them from Cork City alone. Many of them lie buried with hundreds of thousands of other British soldiers in the cemeteries of northern France and Flanders. Cork got a taste of the horrors of the war when the *Lusitania* was sunk off the Old Head of Kinsale on 8 May 1915.

MUNICIPAL GEMS

Mansion House, aka Mercy Hospital

Lifestyles amongst the wealthy classes were lavish in the eighteenth century. A map of 1750 shows a large bowling green with trees planted on its margin located in the newly developed western marshes on the site that would later become the Mansion House. The trees created a shaded walk and music bands played in the area for the entertainment of the wealthy classes. Next to the bowling green was the Assembly House where meetings of the wealthy classes were held two days in the week.

Soon the area became host to the city's Mansion House or what is now the oldest part of Mercy University Hospital. It was built for the Mayor of Cork between 1764 and 1767. Many of the original features are still evident in the hospital today. For example, the female medical ward was originally a reception room and the current physiotherapy unit was once the Mayoral Ballroom. The Minstrels Gallery is still in place, high up on the wall over the doorway to this unit. The architect was an Italian called Davis Ducart who practised architecture and engineering in Ireland in the 1760s and 1770s. He designed several large buildings and engineering projects. He had associations with the canal builders of the time and the mining industry and worked on many projects in the County Tyrone coalfield. In Limerick Ducart produced the plan of plots to be leased in the Georgian extension of the city known as Newtown Pery and also those of the Custom House (1769), now home to the Hunt Museum.

In 1842, Cork Corporation decided that Mansion House was too expensive to maintain and they leased it to a priest anxious to set up a second-level educational establishment. It then became known as St Vincent's Seminary. In 1857, St Vincent's Seminary moved to St Patrick's Place and the Administration of Saints Peter and Paul requested the Vincentians to transfer the lease of the premises to them to provide a hospital for the sick and poor of the city. The cost of conversion from school to hospital was £3,793. Thus, on 17 March 1857, the story of the Mercy University Hospital began. A yearly rent was paid to Cork Corporation until 1927 when the Mercy Sisters bought the property. When Mercy University Hospital first opened its doors, there were forty beds and four sisters worked here. Eight admissions were recorded on the first day.

Cornmarket Street

A corn market was constructed in 1719 overlooking a square that was located on a filled-in portion of a channel of the River Lee (Coal Quay). Unfortunately, the name of this square is not recorded, but it was located on what is now Corn Market Street. Over the centuries, the square grew to become the traditional central market area of the city. It would have been thronged with dealers and customers, purchasing anything from a needle to an anchor. Several stalls still operate here today. During 2011-2012 Cornmarket Street underwent a massive facelift after over €1 million was allocated by Cork City Council for the refurbishment. The street now has the feel of a European outdoor market.

A Sailor's Church

A new church, St Paul's, was constructed in 1723 to provide ecclesiastical services to the many sailors passing through Cork. St Paul's church still exists today, adjacent to Paul Street Shopping Centre, but is now unoccupied. After its construction, ships used to dock at Lavitt's Quay and also at Custom House Quay, now Emmett Place.

In 1720, the town's custom house had been relocated from lower St Patrick's Street to what is now the premises of the Crawford Art Gallery. Part of the 1720 structure is still visible on Emmett Place, adjacent to Cork Opera House. In the grounds of St Paul's church, one can see a large number of sailors' graves. In 1723, Edward Brockelsby, Mayor of the city, granted free burials to all foreign sailors.

The church is simple in style, borrowing largely from the Grecian style. It possesses a pitched roof, is rectangular in plan with random rubble masonry and has no major features externally. Its interior, however, makes up for the absence of exterior adornment. The stuccowork on the ceiling is reputed to be the work of Italian prisoners of war who were captured in Ireland during the Napoleonic Wars. There is an accomplished stained-glass window, depicting the Last Supper. In the vestry are the old wooden stocks, once used to hold criminals while a crowd pelted them with rotten food.

Sirius Business

The City of Cork Steamship Company was established in 1843 under the direction of Ebenezer Pike and was built on the former structure of St George Steampacket Company in England. Its principal building still survives today and the statue of St George slaying a dragon still adorns the top of the building. In the beginning, the Cork company bought older steamships and purchased new ones. Perhaps, the most famous steamship acquired was the *Sirius*, built in 1837 by Menzies & Co., Perth and engineered by J. Wingate & Co., Glasgow. The ship will be remembered for being the first passenger steamship to make the voyage from Europe to America, from London via Cork to New York on 28 March 1838.

Crawford Art Gallery

In 1883 a deputation, consisting of Mr James Brenan, RHA, schoolmaster of the Cork School of Art and the honorary secretary, was sent to London, to request further finance from the Committee of Council for Education, to construct a municipal art gallery.

Several months later, through the efforts of the committee and headmaster, William Horatio Crawford, a prominent Cork City merchant, was persuaded to donate the necessary finance to complete a renovation and extension of the existing School of Art. The cost was £20,000 whilst Arthur Hill of the architectural firm of Hill & Co. designed the renovated building and extension. The firm was renowned in the city for their use of good quality building materials.

It was originally proposed that the extension and additions would include a school of art and science and the wrought-iron gates at the entrance to the Crawford Art Gallery still bear the inscriptions, 'Art' and 'Science'. The roof was to be complete with several turrets. The initial intention was also to have art and technology taught under the one roof with both an art museum and a science museum. However, due to the cost, many of Arthur Hill's designs were scaled down. The exterior roof was to have only one turret, still visible today and which marks the joining of the old eighteenth-century Custom House and the new School of Art and gallery extension. The wrought-iron gates at the entrance to the new school of art and gallery building bear the date 1884, the year the extension and renovation were completed. The official opening ceremony was not held until 15 April 1885.

Casts from the Vatican

In the second decade of the 1800s, the acquisition of the classical casts of Antonio Canova was an important contribution to the cultural status of Cork. Around 1810, Pope Pius VII was anxious to express his gratitude to the English people for the return to the Vatican Galleries of many masterpieces looted by Napoleon

The Canova Cast.

Bonaparte. Thus, the Pope commissioned Italian artist, Antonio Canova, to make a set of over 100 casts from the classical collection in the Vatican. In 1812, the casts were shipped to London as a gift to the Prince Regent, later George IV. The prince showed a lack of appreciation towards his papal acquisitions and they lay firstly in the London Custom House and then in the basement of his residence in Carleton Gardens. Lord Listowel of Convamore, County Cork, a patron of the arts and a friend of the prince, suggested that they should be donated as a gift to the people of Cork. Agreeing, the prince donated them to the Cork Society of Fine Arts, whose premises was located on the intersection of St Patrick's Street and Falkener's Lane.

Shortly afterwards, the Cork Society of Fine Arts suffered financial difficulty and could not pay the rent of the premises in which the casts were kept so they applied to the government for monetary aid. The Westminster government, under the recommendation of the Lord Lieutenant of Ireland, stated they could grant no aid but recommended they amalgamate with the Royal Cork Institution. An arrangement was made that the Royal Cork Institution, an adult education body founded in 1803, should obtain the casts and pay the debt of £500-£600 that was contracted by the Society of Fine Arts. A compromise was made of £300 and the casts were moved to the Institution's premises on Jameson Row. Several of the casts can be viewed today in the Crawford Art Gallery.

Jewtown

Immortalised by the name Jewtown, Albert Road and the area of the Hibernian Buildings have been imbued by the story of Cork's Jewish community. The Cork Jewish Congregation was founded about the year 1725 with Shochet (Jewish official who oversees the kosher slaughter of animals) and cemetery. It comprised Ashkenazi and Sephardi Jews engaged in import and export. By 1871, there were nine Jews in Munster. During the Russian oppression of 1881, several Jews of Vilna, Kovno and Ackmeyan, a Lithuanian village, came to live in Cork. A congregation was formed at the close of 1881 and Meyer Elyan of Zagger, Lithuania, was appointed Shochet, Reader and Mothel. The community had close links with those of Dublin and Limerick.

Several of the earliest arrivals from a cluster of *shtetls* (small towns with a large pious Jewish population) in north-western Lithuania settled in a group of recently constructed dwellings called Hibernian Buildings, Monarea Terrace and Eastville off the Albert Road, around 1880. Much of the streetscape has changed little from when the first Lithuanian Jews arrived. Hibernian Buildings was a triangular development of a hundred or so compact and yellow-brick on-street dwellings. Each unit consisted of four rooms, including a bedroom up in the roof space. About the year 1884, a room was rented in Marlborough Street from the Cork Branch of the National League and a synagogue was fitted up in the offices there. Premises were finally acquired at 24 South Terrace. The number of Jews in the city and county combined rose from twenty-six in the year 1881 to 217 in the year 1891.

The O'Flynn Brothers, based in Blackpool, were responsible for the construction of the Hibernian Buildings as well as the Rathmore Buildings, St Patrick's Hospital, The Good Shepherd Convent, Magdalen Asylum, additions to Our Lady's Hospital, a new presbytery at the North Cathedral, and the Diocesan College at Farranferris.

National Sculpture Factory

In the closing years of the nineteenth century, the Corporation of Cork planned to establish a large electricity generating plant. The plant would provide public lighting and operate an electric tramcar extending from the city centre to all of the popular suburbs. The site of the new plant was on Monarea Marshes (now the National Sculpture Factory) near the Hibernian Buildings. The Electric Tramways and Lighting Company Ltd was registered in Cannon Street, London and had a close working relationship with eminent electrical contractors, the British Thomson-Houston Company. This latter English company was appointed as the principal contractors. The street track was completed by William Martin Murphy, who was a Berehaven man, but with a company in Dublin. William was the first chairman of the Cork company. Leading Cork housing contractor, Edward Fitzgerald, soon to become Lord Mayor of Cork, completed the building of the plant. To provide proper foundations for the large plant, extensive quantities of pitch pine were sunk under the concrete.

Charles H. Merz, one of British Thomson-Houston's up-and-coming engineers, supervised the electric tramcar system. He became the secretary and head engineer for the Cork operation. Charles was a native of Newcastle-upon-Tyne and arrived in Cork during the laying of track and near the completion of the plant. Eighteen tramcars arrived in 1898 for the opening, which occurred on 22 December. Cork was to become the eleventh city in Britain and Ireland to have operating electric trams. Four of the six suburban routes were complete for the line's opening. The eventual termini included Sunday's Well, Blackpool, St Luke's Cross, Tivoli, Blackrock and Douglas.

By 1900, thirty-five electric tramcars operated throughout the city and suburbs. They were manufactured in Loughborough, England and all were double deck in nature, open upstairs with a single-truck design. Most tramcars could hold at least twenty-five people upstairs and twenty downstairs. However, a key rule on the tram was that nobody could sit or stand on the driver's front platform!

As an electricity generating station and tram-house, the building has an important connection with the industrial history of the city. It is of continuing cultural significance through its present use as the National Sculpture Factory. The factory was set up in 1989 by four local artists as a response to a need from artists for a large-scale well-equipped studio space where they could work. The National Sculpture Factory is a national organisation which advances the creation and understanding of contemporary art.

Harry Clarke Windows

The Harry Clarke stained-glass windows form a significant feature of the Honan Chapel in University College Cork (built in 1915). The Honan Chapel is built in a distinctive Hiberno-Romanesque style. James F. McMullen, designer of the Honan Chapel, managed to capture the beauty and striking dignity of the ancient style without producing a mere slavish imitation of any one example. Altogether there are nineteen lights in the church. Eleven of them were designed and made by Harry Clarke and the remaining eight were produced by a number of different artists working in the studio of the late Sarah Purser. The difference in the styles of work of the two artists is immediately noticeable. The work of Sarah Purser is characterised by the use of pale tints throughout and by the naturalistic presentation of the human figure. The Clarke windows, on the other hand are a blaze of rich deep colours and his artistry is strongly embellished with caricature like figures wearing jewelled garments.

This stained glass was Harry Clarke first major commission. It established Clarke as a stained-glass artist of distinction not just in Ireland but also in Western Europe. His eleven Honan Chapel windows were completed in 1917. They depicted Our Lady, Saints Finbarre, Albert, Declan, Ita, Brendan, Gobnait and Joseph and a three-light window of Saints Columcille Patrick and Brigid.

Lifetime Lab

Officially opened in October 2005, the Lifetime Lab, a Cork City Council initiative funded by the European Free Trade Association (EFTA), was a welcome move in protecting and reinvigorating Cork's heritage stock. As with every old city, the problem of what to do with a building whose function has expired is a nightmare for any owner. Formerly, the old Waterworks on Lee Road, the complex has been converted into a 'lab' where visitors of all ages, especially children, can enjoy a modern interactive exhibition, steam plant, beautifully restored buildings, children's playground and marvellous views over our Lee Fields.

The buildings which stand at the waterworks site today date from the 1800s and 1900s but water has been supplied to the city of Cork from the site since the 1760s. A foundation stone today commemorates the building of the first pump-house, which was itself constructed on the Lee Road in the late eighteenth century. It was in 1768, that Nicholas Fitton was elected to carry out the construction work needed for the new water supply plan. The waterwheel and pump sent the river water unfiltered to an open reservoir called the 'City Basin' which was located on an elevated level above the Lee Road. This water was then pumped from here to the city centre through wooden pipes.

Between the years 1856 and 1857, the Corporation obtained a sanction from the parliamentary treasury to acquire a loan of £20,000 to upgrade the Lee Road Waterworks. In February 1857, John Benson's plan for a new waterworks was given to several eminent engineers in London for consultation. Much of it was based on Londoner Thomas Wickstead's 1841 survey and plan for the provision of water to the Cork public in association with the Corporation of Cork. By May 1857, tenders were issued and cast-iron mains were chosen to replace the wooden pipes. They were initially shipped to Cork in 1857 and during the ensuing two years, the pipes were laid down. By February 1859, the pipes from the new waterworks to the military barracks on the old Youghal Road were in place. It was here that a new reservoir was to be constructed. The reservoir itself was to cover ½ hectare. and was 4½m deep with a capacity of 4 million gallons.

The Straight Road

The Carrigrohane Straight Road was built around the late 1830s and early 1840s. Earlier maps, such as Taylor and Skinner's *Maps of the Roads of Ireland* (1776) or the Grand Jury map of 1811, do not show any track or path in this area. However, the first edition of the Ordnance Survey Map (1841-42) shows that work was in progress on the new road linking Cork City with Carrigrohane and Leemount Cross. The Straight Road seemed to be built by 1842. The section as far as Leemount Cross (including Leemount Bridge) may not have been completed until the famine years (1845-50). The building of the Straight Road and its extension on to Leemount Cross changed the traffic pattern to the west of the city. Before the Straight Road and Leemount Bridge were built, the Model Farm Road took traffic to Ballincollig and Macroom while the Lee Road led to Blarney, Coachford and Inniscarra. The original surface of Carrigrohane Straight Road was limestone.

Perhaps the biggest changes to the structure and view of the Carrigrohane Straight Road came in the 1920s and '30s. In 1927, Cork County Council and Cork Corporation, who both controlled sections of the Straight Road, laid reinforced concrete. The Straight Road was one of the first concrete road surfaces in Ireland and one of the first in Great Britain. The South of Ireland Asphalt Company (SIAC) was engaged in the surfacing of the Straight Road and the concrete was hand laid. Three years later, and a few days before the London Motorcycle Exhibition in early November 1930, a new world record attempt was staged on the Carrigrohane Straight Road because of its fine surface. Joseph S. Wright, one of Great Britain's foremost motorcycle racers, travelled to Cork to make the attempt and French officials arrived with special electric timing apparatus. Joseph Wright rode a 1,000cc QEC Temple JAP-engined machine and regained the record by clocking up at just over 150 miles per hour. As a follow up to this event, in 1936, 1937 and 1938, Grand Prix car races were held on the Carrigrohane Straight Road.

5

CRIME AND PUNISHMENT

MEDIEVAL CORK

Life in medieval Cork was harsh and difficult. Various depictions of the walled town show the drawbridge towers topped by the dismembered heads of executed criminals which were placed as a warning to the other citizens contemplating crime. The severed head was placed onto a spike and this was slotted into a rectangular slab of stone. Legend has it that one of the stone blocks still exists and can be seen today at the top of the steps of the Counting House in Beamish and Crawford Brewery on South Main Street. Other methods of execution included being hanged at Gallows Green, a location on the southern valley side near to the southern road leading into town. The site is now marked by Greenmount National School and the Lough Community Centre.

Excavations in 1993 on the site of the medieval abbey at Crosses Green in Cork revealed over 200 skeletons, citizens of the medieval town. Three-quarters of the individuals were found to be adults and the largest number had been aged in their twenties. There were slightly more males than females excavated. Just less than half were found to have degenerative joint disease or some form of arthritis. In several individual skeletons, nutritional deficiencies, tumours, and dental diseases were noted along with infections. It was also observed that some individual skeletons had died because of being involved in physical violence with other people or in an accident. In the case of violence, death was mainly caused by a sword or an axe blow. This was evidenced by the cut marks of such weapons.

Heads on spikes at North Gate Bridge. (Late sixteenth-century map of Cork as depicted in Sir George Carew's *Pacata Hibernia, or History of The Wars in Ireland* vol. 2 (1633).

REBEL CORK

In the late 1400s, English nobles began to fight among themselves as to who should be king. The conflict arose in particular between the House of Lancaster, whose symbol was a red rose, and the House of York, which had a white rose. Known as the Wars of the Roses, the political turmoil came to a conclusion at the Battle of Bosworth in 1485 when the House of Lancaster won. A new king named Henry VII was appointed and he set out straight away to heal the effects of the civil war. However, individuals from the House of York were scheming to overthrow him. One such plot involved the impersonation of Richard Plantagenet, Duke of York and one-time heir to the throne, who had mysteriously vanished after being locked up in the Tower of London. In 1492, a man named Perkin Warbeck, who resembled the duke, was used to rally support for the Yorkists within the walled town of Cork.

Warbeck claimed to be the Duke of York and that he had just escaped from the Tower of London. He was well received and entertained by the citizens, especially by an eminent merchant named John Walters. Walters believed his story and promised to support the Yorkist side. Warbeck also wrote letters to the Earls of Kildare and Desmond in Munster mentioning that in the past they used to support the white rose side and that military assistance would be appreciated. However, before Warbeck could establish a large Irish force, he was called to France by French King, Charles II, who wished to use this impersonation to his advantage against the English crown.

Three years later, in 1495, Warbeck set sail for the Kentish coast with 600 men to gain the English crown. However, his campaign was a disaster and many of his men were caught and executed. Warbeck escaped and came back to Cork but received little assistance. A consequent trip to Scotland to persuade some of the Scots to invade England failed when a peace agreement was drawn up. Whilst in Scotland he married the daughter of the Earl of Huntley but was then forced to flee Scotland with his new family due to the peace agreement.

In July 1497, he came back to Cork and with the aid of the Earl of Desmond enlisted 120 soldiers with the intention of invading the coast of Cornwall. It is reported that on his arrival in Cornwall, he was joined by several thousand other soldiers but he was caught by the opposition and sent to the Tower of London. In 1499, Perkin Warbeck was tried at Westminster and John Walters was also summoned over from Cork to be tried. Both were found guilty of high treason and hanged.

A NEW KING

In April 1603, Queen Elizabeth I died and a new Protestant king, James I, was proclaimed. Captain Morgan was given the responsibility by the Lord Lieutenant of Ireland, Deputy Mountjoy, to relate the news to Cork. In Cork, the message was received by George Thornton, one of the king's appointed commissioners for Munster, who gave the news to the Mayor of Cork, Thomas Sarsfield. Sarsfield was anti the crown and a supporter of the rebellious Irish living in the area. He knew that he could not refuse outright to proclaim the new monarch for fear of military reprisals but decided to use niches in the political system to delay the process of proclamation.

Sarsfield took his right to call together elected officials of Cork Corporation at the city courthouse to decide on the matter. During this time, he was informed that Thornton, the English commissioner, was waiting for a response outside the meeting. Sasfield managed to delay the process further by declaring that the meeting had to be adjourned until the following day. This rebellion of the Irish officials did not deter Thornton from carrying out the proclamation and he and 800 soldiers proclaimed the new king in the north suburbs of the city around Shandon Castle.

Under pressure, Sarsfield and the citizens contemplated attacking a fort at Haulbowline but agreed on arming themselves and preventing any English forces from entering the town. A number of principal characters are recorded in this revolt. One such man, a Thomas Fagan, had an interesting personality. One incident involving Thomas included the time he fired a cannon at an Englishman, James Grant. He had previously attacked Grant and stripped him of his clothes. Fagan was also responsible for breaking into the city's ammunition store within a former towerhouse called Skiddy's Castle. This store was located at the northern end of North Main Street, now the site of the National Rehabilitation Board. However, firing cannons at people and raiding gunpowder stores were only one part of his personality. Fagan also carried a white rod around the city and declared himself the principal churchwarden in the city. It is recorded that any English person or Protestant that passed him was mocked without fail.

Even certain Englishmen took the side of the rebels. John Nicholas, brewer, and John Clarke, tanner, mounted a small portable cannon on top of the walls and fired at two soldiers, killing them. The town's recorder, John Mead was also on the side of the rebellion and used his political clout accordingly. Mead ordered the king's storekeeper, Allen Apsely at Skiddy's Castle, to be killed and his arms to be taken away. He also ordered the arrest of the clerk of the munitions, Michael Hughes, along with his wife who was sentenced to be thrown over the walls as a means of execution for, it seems, an unknown crime.

In May 1603, Mountjoy marched forcefully into the city with a troup of soldiers. The Irish citizens on seeing this brought out their ploughshares and set them on both sides of the street showing their apathy towards the force in particular. The lord lieutenant ignored these obstacles, rounded up the main ringleaders and made examples of them.

SIEGE OF CORK

Cork also played a key part in the Williamite Wars, being one of the Jacobite-held towns and only falling to the Willamite forces in 1690 after heavy bombardment. The principal officers on the Jacobite side of the Siege of Cork were taken away to

King William besieging Cork, 1690, depicted in Mary F.C. Cusack's *A History of the City and County of Cork* (Francis Guy, 1875).

the Tower of London in England to be beheaded. Some of the 4,000-5,000 Jacobite soldiers were taken to be imprisoned in Clonmel while other large numbers were transported to London to be imprisoned. When the siege was over, Col. John Hales replaced Mac Elligott as governor and was presented with the freedom of the town in a silver box from William of Orange. The Duke of Marlborough also received the freedom of the town. Today, there are two visible remnants of this siege in the city. On the corner of the Grand Parade and Tuckey Street, embedded into the pavement, is a cannon that was reputedly used during the siege. It is said that it was later used as a mooring post for a quayside in the 1700s. The second is the cannon ball fired from Elizabeth Fort at the tower of the then St Fin Barre's Cathedral.

MUNICIPAL WATCHMEN

In the early 1740s Mayor Hugh Winter employed fifteen watchmen to walk around the city at night between eleven o'clock and sunrise to protect the citizens. Eleven o'clock was the city's curfew, and any person caught outdoors after that time faced prosecution or expulsion. Robbery was common, with money and clothing often reported missing. Items such as silk, lead and swords were targeted by thieves and the raiding of cellars for food was also common. There were two gaols in the eighteenth-century city, one overlooking South Gate Bridge and the other overlooking North Gate Bridge. These gaols housed debtors and malefactors.

GALLOWS GREEN

Up to 1852 Deerpark Road was known as the Kinsale Road and it terminated at Gallows Green, where all public executions were undertaken until 1868. Greenmount Crescent was then called Gallows Green Lane and when the Cork Corporation leased the lands to the Presentation Brothers to build a school there the street and location names were changed in order to eradicate the distasteful memory of the site's original function.

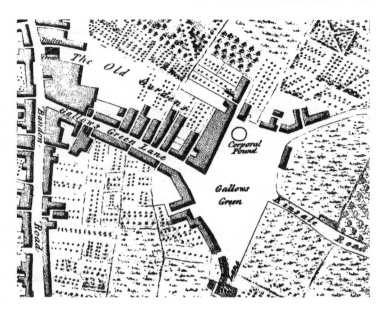

Gallows Green from John Rocque's Map of Cork 1759.

In July 1990 human remains were uncovered in the back garden of a private residence in Greenmount, Cork City. The original ground level of the garden was almost 2 metres higher than the ground level of the house. It was while reducing the level of the garden that bones were discovered. At least fifteen individuals were recovered from the area. None of the skeletons was complete and many of the bones were broken. In one area all the long bones were stacked neatly together with the skulls lying close by.

A Curious Incident

In 1766, the Theatre Royal had a role in a rather unusual event: A tailor named Patrick Redmond was to be hanged on 10 September 1766 for robbing the house of a man called John Griffin. During the execution at Gallows Green (modern-day Greenmount and Bandon Road area in the city) rain was threatening, so the city officials and the civil guard departed after Redmond had been hanging for nine minutes, before confirming that the executioner Jack Ketch had successfully hanged Redmond. Realising that he might still be alive, the tailor's friends carried Redmond to a nearby cabin.

Present at the hanging was a well-known comedian named William Frederick Glover, whose main occupation was that of a surgeon. He volunteered his services and 'proceeded by massage and fumigation' to restore Redmond's circulation. Redmond soon regained consciousness, sat up, and helped himself to a 'proffered bottle of whisky'. After his miraculous feat Glover set off to the Theatre Royal on George's Street, to play his role in a benefit performance on the same night. However, his performance was interrupted:

> The resurrected tailor, drunk as a fool and waving a shillelagh, thrust himself through the orchestra and scrambled onto the stage. Then he shouted: 'Good Christians and Honest People, whatever debt Mr Glover there is talkin' about, 'tis nothin' at all to what I owe him, for sure he saved my life.'

The apparent presence of a dead man on stage caused consternation in the audience, amongst whom was the Sheriff of Cork. One report states that the sheriff simply turned a blind eye to events, while others record that the sheriff called out to seize him. However, Redmond was removed before he could be rearrested and 'Eventually he moved to Dublin to become tailor to the "Corps Dramatique".'

CORK CITY GAOL

The first plan for a new gaol outside the former medieval city was drawn up in 1808 when Cork Corporation decided to alleviate the appalling conditions and overcrowding at the eighteenth-century North Gate Prison. A grant of £20,000 was given by the English Parliament to support its construction in Sunday's Well while Sir Thomas Deane was appointed architect and Mr Richard Natter from Carrigdubh builder. The selected building material was sandstone and this was quarried locally. Building commenced in 1821 and on 17 August 1824, the first prisoners arrived.

Many of the criminals sent to the City Gaol were found guilty of petty crimes. The stealing of clothing, bread, personal possessions and even animals were among the main crimes committed in the city. It was only in April 1828 that the first public execution took place outside the main gate when Mr Owen Ryan was hanged for the crime of rape. Bells tolled and black flags waved in the wind on top of the gaol as Ryan slowly met his demise looked upon by the High Sheriff of the city and the gaol governor.

The gaol itself was governed by a board of superintendence, which was headed by the mayor who then had to report to the city council on all matters arising. An inspector who reported every year to the crown in turn oversaw the council.

The first decade of the life of the gaol witnessed several interesting events. In 1836, the prison was divided into two parts, male and female. On average, approximately 1,600 prisoners were held in the gaol each year. The majority had short stays due to the non-severity of their crime. Hooliganism, larceny, drunkenness and disorderly behaviour were the main offences carried out in the city. The remaining numbers were made up of debtors and nationalist members of the public.

In the 1920s the gaol came to the forefront of Cork's institutions again. Amidst a backdrop of political turmoil in the form of the Irish Civil War, the gaol was used to imprison members of the Irish Republican Army. Graffiti from these men is preserved on the gaol cell walls and can still be seen today. A 1922 report noted that the prison was infested with vermin and had a suicide net hung by the iron stairway. However, it is also stated that gaslights existed in the corridors and radiator pipes in the cells.

After the civil war, the prison closed and the prisoners were transferred to other gaols. In 1927, the gaol became Cork Broadcast Station and in the 1930s, any gaol fittings were sold off in auction. The radio station closed in 1958 and the building was taken over by the Department of Posts and Telegraphs as a training school. Lectures were even given in the cells on the ground floor. However, in the 1970s and 1980s, the gaol was used as a store for poles and drums for the locality. This was eventually phased out in the 1980s. In 1992, work began on turning the gaol into the popular heritage centre it is today.

6

THE WORKING LIFE

MEDIEVAL INDUSTRY

Archaeological evidence indicates the existence of several crafts within medieval Cork. The largest of these seems to be the craft of metal-working. Large quantities of iron slag have been found along with iron-smelting furnaces. The most significant of these was revealed during the placing of foundations for the Gate Cinema in 1994. Here a forge was discovered which had a short life span in the first half of the 1300s.

A substantial amount of iron objects have been found which include, for example; knives, spearheads, nails; horse tack such as horseshoes, bits and spurs; tools such as drill bits, shears, gouges and punches; barrel padlocks and keys. Bronze objects, for example include stick-pins (dress fasteners), buckles needles and keys. During excavations near the town wall in 1984, a thirteenth-century bronze candlestick with foldable legs was discovered which is now on display in the Cork Museum. Lead objects such as weights have also been discovered. Bone manufacture was common in the town too. The underlining marshy soil in the city provided great preservation for bone artefacts such as combs from antlers of deers; antler gaming pieces such as chessmen and dice, bone needles, spindle whorls, bone harp pegs and toggles like those on present-day duffle coats.

Marshy soil also preserves wood. Numerous wooden artefacts have been found on excavated medieval sites in Cork, which also represent the use of several different native tree species. These species were utilised in different ways according to what type of wooden object was needed. For example, oak was favoured for structural purposes and furniture. Ash was used in the creation of bowls due to the fact that it was easy to carve out. Yew was favoured in carving and stave making. Leather artefacts especially footwear, belts, straps and sheaths also form a large portion of the archaeological record. The importance of the leather industry is reflected in the late 1500s when grants were given by Queen Elizabeth I to the guilds of shoemaking, glove-making and tanning. Textiles mainly took the form of woven or spun silk, wool or animal hairs.

CORK'S BEEF SHARE

Cork, as the capital of a province largely given over to cattle rearing, was a great centre for the export of livestock. As early as 1660, the export of cattle was quite considerable. The most important sources of supply were Imokilly, the Lee and Bandon valleys and, above all, the North Cork lowlands. In the early to mid-eighteenth century, Cork merchants possessed the largest share of the Irish export trade in beef. In 1720, Cork merchants exported 58,916 barrels of beef while in 1745, the figure had escalated to 73,594 barrels. The 1745 Cork total represented almost 60 per cent of the full Irish export total.

The importance of beef to the English economy was reflected in 1747 in a Westminster Act, passed by George II, and which related directly to Cork. The Act gave legal powers to the Corporation of Cork exports to inspect any beef to be exported, and to provide a central market for inspection to take place, hence the name Cattle Market Avenue.

In 1748, two English gentlemen touring Ireland noted that 90,000 black cattle were killed for export purposes between August and December in the City's Cattle Market near Shandon Street. In the western hemisphere, the West Indies provided the greatest market for provisions. Other export areas were Barbados, Carolina, Georgia, Jamaica, Newfoundland and Britain.

THE NEATLY FITTED CITY OF GOODS

In 1732, Edward Lloyd, an English writer, detailed that the population of the city was 40,000 and that the shops in the main core of the city were 'neatly fitted and sorted with rich goods'. In addition, there was a lot of new buildings being constructed and others were being re-constructed.

Newspaper reports, especially from the *Corke Journal*, detail that there was a large array of goods available in the shops of the city and a substantial amount of services were provided. For example, these included drapers, ironmongers, spirit dealers, goldsmiths and jewellers.

Drapery stores sold goods such as silk handkerchiefs, leather gloves and ivory combs. Jewellers sold goods such as gold and silver spurs, buckles and watches while ironmongers dealt in iron locks, grates, nails, hinges and numerous other metal objects. There were even services for the more refined and conservative need. For example, hairdressing plus wig-making was a service provided for those involved in official civic duties, for example in the court.

South Mall Quays, 1843. (*Illustrated London News*)

FIRST FOR CHOICE

By the mid-1700s, the native butter industry in Cork had grown to such an extent that it was decided among the main city and county butter merchants that an institution be established in the city that would control and develop its potential – the 'Committee of Butter Merchants'. Locating themselves in a simple commissioned building adjacent to Shandon, the group consisted of twenty-one members who were chosen by the merchants in the city.

In May 1770, it was decided by the Cork Committee that all butter to be exported from Cork was to be examined by appointed inspectors who had two main duties to perform. Firstly, they had to examine and determine the quality and weight of the butter. Secondly, they had to examine and report on the manner of packing and to detect and signs of fraud. On examination of the casks, the quality of butter was determined and they are awarded a 'first', 'second', 'third', 'fourth', 'fifth', or 'sixth'. 'First' was termed 'superfine' (excellent quality) while sixth butter was termed 'grease' (very poor quality). A penalty was imposed on the inspector if he or she made a poor judgement or was in a conspiracy with a merchant.

If one was a farmer involved in the butter industry, one brought one's butter or hired a broker to bring one's butter from the country to the butter market in the town. It did not matter at what time a farmer or a broker arrived with your butter as the market was open night and day. This was to facilitate sellers and perhaps to avoid concentrating business during mornings or afternoons. On arrival, a porter received the firkin or cask of

Cork butter market, 1858. (*Illustrated London News*)

butter, initialised it, chalked each cask and arranged them into lots so that they could be inspected the following day.

'Cork Firsts' were nearly always sent to Lisbon while 'Cork seconds' were sent to the West Indies. 'Cork Thirds' were sent to Southern England and to certain Scottish Ports. A butter cask had to be made from seasoned oak, sycamore or beech. Oak was particularly useful for preserving butter on long-distance voyages. All firkins being shipped to places like Brazil and the West Indies via certain English ports were also bound in iron hoops and a small portion of butter was taken out to allow for pickle to be included which acted as a preservative of taste.

By the mid-1800s, the butter market had enlarged to such an extent that there was an urgent need for expansion of the premises and, in 1849, an elaborate Classical-style portico, designed by Sir John Benson, was added to the front of the butter market. However, in the late nineteenth century, there was a distinct decline in the economic fortunes of the city. The profits of the export provision trade of agricultural products such as butter and beef declined. In 1858, 428,000 firkins of butter had been exported but by 1891 this was reduced to 170,000 firkins. Competitive European prices undercut the prices set by the butter market at Cork. Eventually, the Cork Butter Market closed in 1924.

THE LARGEST BREWERY IN IRELAND

Adjacent to South Gate Bridge was the world-renowned brewing business of Beamish and Crawford. Before the European Industrial Revolution in the late eighteenth century, many small retailers hindered the development of the brewing industry. They were unfortunately technically out of date and were out-competed by larger native manufacturers in Ireland. This was to change in the closing decade of the eighteenth century when the regulations on the export of Cork's brewed porter were lifted. William Beamish and William Crawford established their porter brewery in 1792 on a site in Cramer's lane that had been used for brewing since at least 1650 (and possibly as early as 1500). Beamish and Crawford's 'Cork Porter Brewery' prospered, and by 1805 it had become the largest brewery in Ireland and the third largest in the then United Kingdom as a whole. In 1805 its output was 100,000 barrels per annum – up from 12,000 barrels in 1792. It remained the largest brewery in Ireland until it was overtaken by Guinness in 1833.

Beamish and Crawford was located by the river for easy accessibility of transport and for a reliable water supply. Associated with these brewing establishments were various storehouses and malt drying houses, which in many established cases were distributed outside the bounds of the brewery in other parts of the city.

AN INDUSTRIAL HUB

Blackpool was the scene of industry in Cork in the eighteenth and nineteenth centuries. In this district, various attempts were made at different times to start or revive the manufacture of textiles such as broadcloth, blankets, flannels, hosiery, thread, braid and rope. The leather industry was also vibrant in Blackpool with no fewer than forty-six tanyards at work there in 1837, giving employment to over 700 hands and tanning on average 110,000 hides annually. From 1835 onwards tanners found it necessary to import hides from as far afield as Montevideo and Gibraltar in order to supplement local supplies.

Richard Griffith's Evaluation of 1852 listed twenty-one tanneries in the Blackpool area. By the turn of the twentieth century only a handful remained in production. The main tannery was Dunn's on the Watercourse Road. One of the most extensive tanyards in Cork belonged to Daniel, fourth son of Jeremiah Murphy and was located in Blackpool. The firm of Daniel Murphy & Sons was not affected by the decline, which ruined many tanning enterprises following the 1830s. A partnership merged with the firm of Dunn Brothers and the new firm became the largest tanning concern in the country at the time. However, the Famine dealt the industry a very serious blow from which it never recovered. From that time onwards, the industry steadily declined.

Distilling became significant in the Cork region only during the last decades of the eighteenth century. Hewitt's Watercourse Distillery was established in 1792 by Thomas Hewitt, John

Teulon (both butter merchants) and Richard Blunt (a London distiller). By 1794 the production and sale of whiskey had begun. In 1834 the Hewitt family took sole ownership of the distillery and sold it to the Cork Distillers Company in 1868. By 1876, distilling had ceased at the Watercourse Distillery, although the maltings, cornstores and warehouses were still used by the company.

Blackpool is also the home of Lady's Well Brewery, which takes its name from a famous well nearby, which was founded in 1854 by Messrs. James, William, Jerome and Francis Murphy. They formed a private limited company in 1884. The undertaking was remarkably successful. Up-to-date appliances were introduced into every department and no pains were spared to place the brewery amongst the best equipped in Ireland and Britain.

A FISHERMAN'S VILLAGE

In August 1843, a report entitled the 'Physical and Moral Condition of the Working Classes in the Parish of St Michael Blackrock near Cork' was read by North Ludlow Beamish, President of the Cork Scientific and Literary Society, before the statistical section of the British Association of the Advancement of Science at Cork. The population of Blackrock and its immediate environs in April 1843 was 2,630 consisting of 557 families living in 413 houses. Ninety families were living in one-roomed houses, 260 in two rooms and 207 in three or more rooms. The trades Beamish listed were varied: brick makers (numbering 56), cabinet makers (2), carpenters (15), coopers (3), farmers (53), fishermen (111), gardeners (32), gingle drivers (13, generally owners), lime burners (18), masons (14), male servants (79), shoemakers (14), slaters (12), smiths (9), tailors (10). Male children numbered 426. As for females, their total was 1,133 with 372 employed as servants or working in fields. Female children, aged and infirm numbered 453 whilst 305 were unemployed. Beamish noted that wages for tradesmen were on average 20s per week; labouring men received 5s 10d; women 3s and children 2s per week but many able bodied men worked for 5s a week. In time of harvest, good reapers could be got at the ordinary wages of 1s a day.

Blackrock Castle. Section of a painting by Nathanial Grogan, *c.* 1790 (Crawford Art Gallery, Cork)

COOPERS AND BARRELS

In the census of Cork in 1871, there were over 439 coopers in the city and 289 in the county, aged twenty years or over. In the early decades of the nineteenth century, the provision trade had decreased, especially in the butter trade. Thus numbers in the coopering trade had dwindled. However, in the 1850s, this trend changed to become upward and the dairy industry became profitable again. But unemployment still existed and, in an attempt to overcome the problem a delegate meeting was held on 26 July 1870. Two men were sent to the country to gauge any outstanding issues relating to the firkin trade and discourage making coopers of boys not coopers' sons. Association with the Cork City branch was also encouraged. The following month, a stock count was taken of firkins in Cork and on seeing a surplus, an 'idle week' was proposed in the society of the trade. It was proposed that the manufacture of firkins be stopped for a week, so the surplus could be lessened. The proposal was successfully carried by a delegate meeting.

As the year 1870 progressed, stocks continued to be monitored, in order to regulate the amount of available work and delegations were despatched to various centres throughout County Cork in order to encourage tighter organisation in the cooper trade. In addition, a restriction was placed on apprenticeships, which could now only be taken up by cooper's sons. This rule had been in existence but had been relaxed by 1870. Being in contact with coopers in the countryside also meant that existing wage levels and trade practices within the city and the county could be maintained and improved. Wages in the country towns were much lower than in the city for making firkins (three pence versus four pence). At the beginning of 1871, unemployment in the trade was evidenced by the cooper's society demand that all men at work pay one shilling to help pay the idle men.

ELECTRICITY COMETH

In the 1880s, talk of a proposed new electric tramline in Cork arose during the Christian Brothers' Exhibition of the winter of 1889. Held in the Cork Corn Exchange (now the site of Cork City Hall), the key organiser was Revd Brother Dominic Burke, a Christian Brother. Leading up to the event Brother Burke was a leading educationalist in the city with a keen interest in all scientific matters. He lived and taught at the North Monastery School. He had been following Thomas Edison's developments in the USA with electric light with interest. On the occasion of Pope Pius IX celebrating the silver jubilee of his episcopacy, Brother Burke erected a large working lamp bulb in the grounds of the North Monastery. Corkonians were much intrigued by the event.

Brother Burke became friends with Gerald Percival, founder of Cork's first firm of commercial electrical contractors or magnetic engineers as he called himself. Gerald Percival was a Unitarian or a non-subscribing Presbyterian of the Church on Princes Street where he was treasurer and honorary warden. Both Brother Burke and Gerald Percival agreed to work together to develop the concept of electricity in Cork.

The Christian Brothers Exhibition at the city's corn exchange, opened by Catholic Bishop O'Callaghan on 22 October 1889, was an ideal event to promote international science and to call for funds for the establishment of technical education schools in Cork. It included many new scientific apparatus that had not been seen before by the general populace, perhaps the highlight being an electric operating tramcar with eight wheels, which ran around the stalls and sideshows of the vast hall. A dynamo generated the electric current for the electric tramcar. A straight upright pole, rising from the car made contact with the overhead cable. The seed of interest was planted.

FORD AND THE MARINA

In November 1916, Ford motor manufacturers made an offer to purchase the freehold of the Cork Park Race Course Grounds and considerable land adjoining the river near the Marina. Fords, Cork Corporation and the Harbour Commissioners entered into formal negotiations. The company acquired approximately 52 hectares of land, which also had a river frontage. The factory gave employment to at least 2,000 men who were paid the minimum wage of one shilling per hour.

The plant was specially designed for the manufacture of an Agricultural Motor Tractor, well known as the 'fordson', a 22 horse

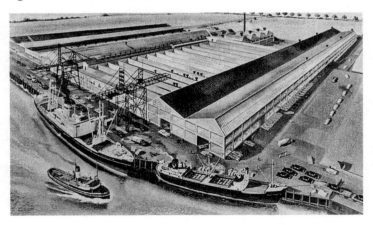

The Ford Plant, unknown artist, *c.*1930.

power, four-cylinder tractor, working with kerosene or paraffin, adaptable either for ploughing or as a portable engine arranged for driving machinery by belt drive. The demand for such tractors was universal and great. Large areas could be brought under food production with the minimum of expense and labour. The Cork factory was to provide 'Fordsons' to local, regional and national farmers and further afield on the European Continent.

In the decade of the 1950s, Ford consistently captured between 25 per cent and 35 per cent of the Irish car market, and between 35 and 40 per cent of the Irish commercial vehicle market. It had an impressive record – by taking passenger and commercial vehicles together, it was the best market share of any Ford company in the world.

The Cork Ford Plant subsequently turned out the widest range of vehicles under one badge on the Irish market, with some fourteen different passenger models and a wide selection of commercials. The total Ford area covered 52 hectares and the growth of the factory increased more than 200 per cent in the decade between 1956 and 1966. By 1967, it had about 1,000 employees assembling cars and commercial vehicles for use throughout the Republic. It continued to prosper for many years but due to pressures of national and global markets and increased competition it closed in 1984.

A RUBBER EMPIRE

The Dunlop Rubber Company (Ireland) Ltd was incorporated on 24 March 1924. An article in the *Cork Examiner* of 16 November 1927 reveals that the company decided to open a large distribution depot in Cork for the southern trade. To suit their purpose they erected a large brick and ferro-concrete structure at the Lower Glanmire Road adjacent to Kent Station. The storage space of the building amounted to 9,000 square feet (2,743 square metres). A hydro-electric solid tyre-fitting press was installed and a compressor for giant tyres. A full range of pneumatic and solid motor tyres, and all accessories, were stocked. Goods manufactured by the subsidiary companies of the Dunlop group were to be stocked at Dunlop House, which included waterproof garments, rubber goods, and sporting requisites. The distribution depot manager was T.W. Kerrigan, former assistant Irish manager and southern representative of the company, who had a twenty-five-year connection with the motor and cycle business.

In 1934, the Irish Dunlop Co. Ltd became a public company and commenced manufacturing at a new factory, leasing a building from Ford on the Marina. The then Minister for Industry and Commerce Seán Lemass TD made a deal with Dunlop to entice them to set up a factory whereby the company would have an 80 per cent share of tyre production in the Irish Free State.

In 1947 Dunlop's lease on the Marina factory in Cork was due to expire so in April that year they agreed to purchase it from Ford for £260,000. By this time the factory had grown to cover nearly 200,000 square feet (610 square metres) and fronted a deep-water berth on the River Lee.

By the 1960s many Irish households and Irish industrial and commercial projects were dependent on Dunlop to a large or minor extent. An article in the *Irish Press* by journalist Liam Flynn on 23 April 1962 reminded readers that the company produced 35,000 golf balls a year and tennis balls were coming onto the market from Cork at the rate of 6,000 dozen a year. Footwear had leaped from 730,000 pairs in 1936 to 1,500,000 pairs in 1961. Although Dunlop supplied the entire country, the output far exceeded the demands and so much of the production of the Marina factory was exported to Britain and Germany and further afield to South Africa, Pakistan and the Unite States. Despite the Cork work's connection with the massive worldwide organisation, the Irish section of 2,500 employees was manned almost exclusively by Irish personnel.

By the 1980s the company was under pressure due to market decline and it closed its doors in 1984.

FORWARD LOOKING

Over the past twenty-five years, Cork has attracted many of the world's largest companies to locate within the region and is now home to global market leaders in pharmaceuticals, healthcare,

ICT, biotechnology, professional services and international financial services.

A competitive business environment offering corporation tax rates of 12.5 per cent for trading, Cork is the chosen European manufacturing and services location for the worldwide operations of such major corporations as Pfizer, Novartis, GlaxoSmithKline, Eli Lily, Schering Plough, Apple Inc., Boston Scientific, Stryker, Johnson & Johnson, EMC, Amazon, Bank of New York Mellon and Citco.

Cork is a dynamic, research-oriented university city with a third-level student population (UCC and CIT) in excess of 35,000 students. Cork also possesses a number of world-renowned research institutes such as the Tyndall National Research Institute focusing on photonics, electronics, materials, nanotechnologies and ICT; the Alimentary Pharmabiotic Centre pioneering the disciplines of gastrointestinal health; Moorepark Dairy and Food Research Centre, in addition to six of the twenty significant green research centres on the island of Ireland.

With an international airport and a thriving passenger and cargo port, Cork enjoys direct access to European destinations and to the principal European hubs such as London, Brussels, Amsterdam and Paris, making it a strategic gateway to Europe. Similarly, Cork is linked to Dublin via a high-quality motorway, and plans are in progress to connect Cork to the cities of Limerick and Galway via a similar motorway corridor. Cork is also serviced by a modern and frequent intercity rail link and commuter rail service.

Cork Harbour is Europe's largest natural harbour and the Port of Cork utilises this asset by providing Ireland's only multipurpose deep-sea port facility. The port provides direct Ro-Ro services to Scandinavia, the Mediterranean and West Africa in addition to frequent ferry services to the UK and France. The port also has significant development plans for a new port facility on the lower harbour, which will have the capacity to handle some of the largest vessels in the world. This is a significant advantage to companies involved in manufacturing as it facilitates the efficient and timely transport of goods globally.

7

POVERTY, FAMINE AND EMIGRATION

LIFE IN MEDIEVAL CORK

Overcrowding in Medieval Cork was common and houses were on the most part poorly ventilated with thatched roofs and clay floors, which was an attraction to rats and fleas. The upper floors of these residences often projected out, blocking the light to the street below. The streets and laneways were therefore gloomy at the best of times along with being ill paved and very mucky due to tidal water seeping up through the marshy islands. The water supply was always subject to contamination from sewage and household rubbish thrown onto the streets and laneways. Dead animals were left to decay where they fell and clothing and hair provided shelter from fleas and lice. It is no surprise then that diseases were rife. These included: measles, mumps, influenza, leprosy, chicken pox, scarlet fever, tuberculosis, typhus and whooping cough.

Diseases usually preyed largely on children and the elderly. As a result, one fifth of all new-born babies died before their first birthdays. Only half of all children survived to adulthood. In the mid-1300s, a European plague known as the Black Death swept through the town. This was a plague carried by fleas that bred on rats. These rats managed to find their way onto ships destined for Cork from the European mainland. In addition, due to English nobles in England fighting over who should be King, there were major shortages of food throughout the 1400s and 1500s. Thus, malnutrition was rife and became a catalyst for disease to spread faster.

POPULATION BOOM

The mid-to-late eighteenth century witnessed many new challenges for a rapidly changing city like Cork. Whereas the merchant class was enjoying the profits of growing trade links, life in Cork for the lower classes was not easy. By 1730, the population had grown to 56,000, by 1750 to 73,000 and by 1790, the population of the urban area was 73,000. This was a large increase from a population of 20,000 100 years previously.

The rapid population growth caused problems for the poorer working-class person. In 1750 historical writer Charles Smith recorded that the inhabitants of Cork were obliged to drink polluted water and that smallpox was very common amongst the people. Other concerns included the dirt and heaps of mud and dung lying in the streets, lanes and alleys. The filth began to be dealt with in the 1780s when fines were placed on illegal dumping. Scavengers, wheelbarrow men and street sweepers

Water's Lane by C. Masom, taken from Mary F.C. Cusack's *A History of the City and County of Cork* (Francis Guy, 1875).

were appointed in the 1790s. Many of the city's structures also were in decay and needed much repair.

Among these, some of the lanes in the old medieval core needed to be revamped. Castle Street was widened in 1791 while in 1795 it was suggested that North and South Main Street were in need of repair.

In 1765, a commission had been set up to deal with the problems of an expanding city. Known as the Wide Street Commission, their primary job was to widen these laneways and therefore get rid of some of the health problems attached to them. They also aimed to lay out new streets. Sixteen commissioners were appointed in Cork in 1765, but due to financial problems it was really only in the early 1800s that they made an impact. About this time, streets such as South Terrace, Dunbar Street and Washington Street, then known as Great Georges Street (opened November 1824), were laid out. Streets such as Shandon Street were also widened.

THE HOUSE OF INDUSTRY

As the early nineteenth century progressed, the increased wealth of the middle and upper classes associated with Cork's trade led to an increase in the construction of churches and secular buildings, reflecting the growing number of institutions in the city. For the poorer classes, Cork was socially a very unstable place. A failing economy had created much unemployment and thus poverty. Epidemics such as typhus swept through the city in 1819 and cholera in 1832. Throughout these years, there were numerous public meetings, to discussed the poverty situation. These meetings did provoke some improvements: the north and south gaols were demolished and it was suggested that Cork Corporation construct new city sewers, which were accessible to the tides. Demand also increased for public toilets by the river.

The House of Industry was opened in 1777 in Blackpool and aided some of the worst-off citizens through times of distress, destitution and epidemics. But it was often packed to capacity. Some of the inmates were obliged to sleep in the open and large numbers were turned away each day. There was also overcrowding at the city's fever hospital. The resources of the House of Industry were often stretched to the limit. Indeed, it was only through the personal contributions of its officials that is was possible to keep it in operation through the 1830s. In 1831, there were 1,810 inmates with 340 lunatics. In 1833 a report recorded that four to six were crammed in a bed and that the main categories of inmates were: 'sick, sore, halt, lame, blind, friendless, hopeless, aimless and wretched'. A survey of the city parishes at the same time revealed in the summer of 1832 that 21,000 people were destitute in Cork.

THE FIRST WORKHOUSE

When the Irish Poor Relief Act was passed on 31 July 1838, the Assistant Poor Law Commissioner, William J. Voules, came to Cork in September 1838 to organise the implementation of the new Act. Meetings were held in towns throughout the county. Cork was divided into twelve wards and thirteen electoral areas in the remaining parts of new Cork Union. He chose the House of Industry as the site of the new Cork Workhouse. Voules noted that there was a problem of migration into the city due to rural

Capstan mill at the workhouse. (Unknown artist, Cork City and County Archives)

people being driven into the settlement by poverty. He also argued that the new workhouse needed much funds and restructuring regarding the set of workhouse rules. However, twenty guardians were elected and funds were advanced from the city's Provincial Bank and a number of governors. Inmates from outside the Cork area were sent to their home places. In February 1840, the House of Industry was formally taken over by guardians and became known as Cork Union Workhouse.

By July 1840, there were 1,750 inmates. The board of guardians held regular meetings. Discussions at these meetings were aimed at improving the composition of the Workhouse Declaration. This included improving admission practices, the classification system of paupers, and the discipline and education of inmates. In addition, suggestions about diet were also discussed. There was strict classification and confinement of inmates to their own wards. This was to keep order and discipline. In the city, much of the impoverished were on the verge of starvation. Clothing and bedding were pawned and there was much uncertainty and fear over the scarcity of employment and a poor harvest in the city's agricultural hinterland.

Due to overcrowding, a new workhouse was built on Douglas Road on Cork's southside. In 1841 '8 acres, 1 rood and 23 perches' were leased to the Poor Law Guardians from Daniel B. Foley, Evergreen House, Cork. Foley retained an acre, on which was Evergreen House with its surrounding gardens, which fronted South Douglas Road. The subsequent workhouse that was built on the leased lands was opened in December 1841. It was an isolated place, built beyond the city's tollhouse and tollgates. The Douglas Road Workhouse was also one of the first of over 130 workhouses to be designed by the Poor Law Commissioners' architect, George Wilkinson.

THE GREAT FAMINE

In the autumn of 1845, the poverty situation began to escalate to a new level. At this time, reports of potato plight could be heard in many parts of the country and were soon found in crops near the city. As the majority of both the wealthy and poor depended largely on this crop as a staple diet, large-scale worry began to set in. By January 1846, the supply of potatoes had decreased to less than half the previous year's figure and prices had vastly increased. This created social upheaval across the country and led to the establishment of relief committees. In the case of Cork City, the Cork Relief Committee was officially established in April 1846 and bought sacks of Indian meal from the government store and sold them at cheaper prices to the public. The committee met twice a week, and by the end of April, the public had subscribed £3,000 to them.

As well as their meetings, there were also public meetings where employment schemes and food distribution were discussed. Apart from seeking food, they also sought financial assistance to start relief schemes such as additional city markets and the development of a new park on the reclaimed marshes that were located behind the Navigation Wall, now the area of Centre Park Road and the former site of Ford. Several projects were passed. These included creating a wide path around the Lough. The original plan was an encircling road but this idea was dismissed by the works committee. A new road was constructed from the Lough to Pouladuff road, and there was

Famine emigrants, Cork Quays, 1851. (*Illustrated London News*)

stone-breaking at the new park (now Pairc Uí Chaoimh area) and white-washing schemes were also instigated. By the second week of May 1846, the Relief Committee was providing work for 160 men.

By November 1846, there were ten relief depots dispersed across the city and each day 25,000 people were supplied with yellow and white meal. However, employment for the destitute was still scarce and the relief committee had 700 men on their records seeking work and city officials recorded 5,000 half-starved, impoverished people begging on the streets. As the winter progressed, discussion began on establishing soup kitchens. The Society of Friends had applied for permission to use part of the north Main Street market for such a project. The preference by the Cork Relief Committee was that soup kitchens should be run by local parish committees. Within hours of the soup kitchen opening, 400 gallons were disposed of at a halfpenny per quart. Three thousand pints of soup were distributed locally each day and by mid-December, the Cork Relief Committee had established the Southern and Central Soup Depot Committee who had set up two soup outlets. By the end of December, five soup depots were operating.

THE TALE OF ANNIE MOORE

In the late 1840s and early 1850s, the city was one of the principal ports that witnessed large numbers of people boarding ships to America, Australia and Britain. Between 1845 and 1855, 1.5 million departed Ireland for good. In 1845, emigration was at the pre-famine rate of 50,000. It peaked in 1847 when 250,000 left. By 1855, the rate was down to 70,000 per year but emigration from Cork was to continue through the latter half of the nineteenth century.

One such emigrant was Annie Moore from Rowland's Lane in Shandon. The seventeen-year-old girl was travelling with her two younger brothers, Anthony and Phillip, on the SS *Nevada*. The ship had departed from Queenstown on 20 December 1891, carrying 148 steerage passengers. The trio spent twelve days at sea, including Christmas Day, arriving in New York on Thursday evening, 31 December. With Annie leading the way, they were processed through Ellis Island the following morning, New Year's Day. All three Moore children were soon reunited with their parents who were already living in New York City.

EPIDEMICS OF A CITY

A report in 1896 by the labouring classes stated that there were 1,800 tenement houses with high rents, a tenth of which had no backyards and, on average, nearly thirteen people lived in one house. Epidemics such as smallpox, enteric fever, typhus, tuberculosis were all common at the turn of the twentieth century in Cork. In the 1870s and 1880s, Gladstone's Liberal Party in Britain attacked several Irish problems with a range of radical legislation. For example, the introduction of the Irish Land Act attempted to secure fair rents and fixity of tenure for Ireland's large peasant population. In 1874 and 1878 the Public Health (Ireland) Act was passed which meant Cork Corporation also became an urban sanitary authority. Water supply and sewage disposals were the first on their agenda to be improved.

In 1875 and 1879, Acts named the Artisans and Labourers Dwellings Improvements Acts and later the Housing of the Working Classes Act of 1890 detailed the importance of clearing slums. However, at this time no large financial aid was available to carry out large-scale clearance. However, Cork Corporation did make an effort. In 1886, in Blackpool, on the site of an old cattle market, seventy-six new houses were built. Named the Madden's Buildings, these new houses were to set the scene for a further three housing schemes before the turn of the 1900s. These comprised of Ryans' Buildings built in 1888 (sixteen houses in all), the Horgans' Buildings built in 1891 (126 houses in all) and the Roches' buildings in 1892 (128 houses in all).

HOPE FOR THE IMPOVERISHED

In 1926 *Cork, A Civic Survey* mapped out three clearly dilapidated housing areas of Cork – one west of Shandon Street, the north-western corner of the city centre island, and the property to the south-west of St Fin Barre's Cathedral. Except for parts of the northern area, all three were older parts of the city. The survey noted that there was not that much dilapidated property on the island to the east of North Main Street but those houses should be cleared out at the earliest opportunity, and no housing rebuilding undertaken in the area; the space should be fully allocated for shopping and business purposes. The survey also questioned whether residential rebuilding should take place in the low-lying and flood-prone neighbourhood of Henry Street and Grattan Street.

The survey also noted that in the city there were 12,850 houses, inhabited by 15,469 families, giving an average of about five persons in a family and six persons per house. However, nearly one-ninth of the population was crowded into tenements and small houses. There were 719 tenements, housing 8,675 people comprising 2,928 families. In some tenements as many as twelve families lived in a house meant for one family.

In the Civic Survey classification, 2,499 people or 839 families lived in 194 'first-class tenement structures', buildings which appeared to be structurally sound; they were not in good repair but were capable of being put in good repair. Some 6,114 people or 2,038 families lived in 512 second-class tenements, buildings which were so decayed or so badly constructed as approaching the borderline of being unfit for human habitation. While 222 people or sixty-one families lived in thirteen third-class tenements, houses unfit for human habitation and incapable of being rendered fit for human habitation. In the small house category, there were 9,649 people living in 2,329 second-class houses and 211 people living in fifty-four third-class houses.

The survey acknowledged that the task of redistributing people was so large that it might take years to accomplish (which it did). It was hoped, however, that the progress would be more rapid than in Liverpool, where it took twenty years to demolish and rebuild a similar number of houses. One of the chief aims of the survey was that the rebuilding should not be done piecemeal as a series of isolated schemes, but as part of a general scheme of town planning and redistribution of the population.

The site for new social housing chosen on the north side of the city was Gurranabraher. Compulsory-purchase orders were enforced and the required land was obtained and the first 200 houses were officially opened and blessed in March 1934. The outbreak of the Second World War was to break the continuity of development, which spanned the late nineteenth and the early twentieth centuries. It was to be well into the 1940s before development resumed again. The Second World War hampered developments in Cork during the period 1939-1945. In 1944, Manning Robertson produced a development plan but many of his interesting ideas were never implemented due to his death a year after the report was published. The plan outlined that since 1934, a total of 1,876 houses were built by the Corporation, all on healthy sites, involving the transfer of over 10,800 people from unhealthy, overcrowded areas.

8

LEISURE AND ENTERTAINMENT

A STROLL IN THE MARDYKE

In 1719, a large section of marshy land, now the area of Fitzgerald's Park was bought by the town clerk Edward Webber, a Dutchman. Edward decided to build a raised walkway across the marshes at his own private expense. This consisted of a bank walled on both sides and filled up. He named the walkway after a promenade in Amsterdam called the 'Meer-Dyke', which means an embankment to protect the land from the sea. While constructing the walk he also built a tea house of red bricks, which was the first of its kind in Cork. Fruit gardens and pathways of gravel were put down along with stone seats for the convenience of the public. The reputation of Webber's tea house grew and soon it became a place that people of high social status met. After the death of Edward in 1735, his tea house and gardens continued to prosper for over two centuries but eventually closed in the mid-1940s.

ALONG THE MARINA

The Marina was a Victorian walkway funded by Cork Corporation but the original designer is unknown. It aimed to take the citizens away from the pressures of the city centre. Originally, the walkway was a dock called the Navigation Wall, which was a narrow wall constructed in the 1780s that jutted out into the river. The Navigation Wall acted as an extension to the city's docks. Later, gravel and mud were dredged from the river to reclaim the adjacent slobland and create the very popular 'Marina Walk'. The Marina was lined with mature trees, which still exist and the changing colours of the leaves are always a great indicator to the changing seasons in Cork. Eventually, after full reclamation, Cork Park Racecourse was opened in 1869 in the vicinity. In 1917, Ford opened a factory on the site, which closed its doors in 1984. Cork City Council are currently planning for a new residential quarter and employment hub in the docklands.

THE DRAMATIC CITY

The first reference to a theatre in eighteenth-century Cork occurred in 1713 when the directors of Smock Alley Theatre Dublin, Messrs. Joseph Ashbury, Thomas Elrington, John Evans and Thomas Griffith leased property in the marshes to the east of the walled town, now the area of Oliver Plunkett Street. The directors converted a large room into a playhouse. This was the first Smock Alley Theatre outside Dublin. The associated company of actors of the Smock Alley Theatre performed there for two decades during the summer months. At the beginning of the 1730s, a decision was taken by directors of the Cork

Theatre Royal, Cork. (*Illustrated London News*)

Theatre to design a new, purpose-built playhouse. This was to be more suited to the needs of performers and audience. Funds to construct the new Cork Theatre came from the estate of Thomas Elrington who died in Dublin in 1732.

With increasing wealth and elegance came a proposal in 1759 from the management of the Crow Street Theatre Dublin, headed by Spranger Barry, to create a playhouse more fitting of Ireland's second city. The new building was located three blocks east of the old Theatre Royal on the same side of George's Street between Morgan's Lane (now Morgan Street) and Five Alley Lane (now Pembroke Street). The Cork General Post Office now occupies the site. The playhouse façade on George's Street possessed a ground floor-arcade or a façade similar to that of the Crow Street theatre. The Theatre Royal, finished in early summer 1760, was 41½m long and 18m wide, making it the biggest playhouse in eighteenth-century Ireland outside Dublin.

During the eighteenth century, a number of small actor companies established new playhouse venues in Cork's expanding urban area. However, none stood the test of time and many closed within a decade.

A fire gutted the Theatre Royal in 1840, but it was reopened in 1853. In 1875, owner James Scanlan sold the Cork Theatre Royal on Oliver Plunkett Street to the postal authorities who were to use the building as the city's General Post Office. On 10 April 1875, the last three professional performances that were to take place in the Theatre Royal were announced in the *Cork Examiner*. These performances were: Monday 11 April, *Virginius*; Tuesday 12 April, *Hamlet*; Wednesday 13 April, *Belpheggar*. After a period of 113 years, from 1760 to 1875, James Scanlan shifted the centre of theatrical interest to a building at the side of the northern branch of the River Lee, which had been variously known as the Athenaeum, Munster Hall and the city's arts venue.

SITTING IN THE GODS

The iron and glass built Athenaeum began life as an exhibition hall. It was designed by John Benson for the 1852 National Exhibition. In the months after the exhibition, the President of the Royal Cork

Institution, Thomas Tobin formed a committee for converting the use of the Great Exhibition Hall to a venue for promoting culture, the fine arts and practical sciences. The building was transferred from its site overlooking the south channel of the River Lee to the present-day site of Cork Opera House overlooking the north channel of the Lee. As a lecture and assembly hall, the uses of the Athenaeum were limited and in 1874, when the ownership of the building came into the hands of James Scanlan, he remodelled it and added a 700-seat concert hall. In addition, he changed the name to the Munster Hall or Halls. Remodelling made stage performances far more practical but the premises was more suited to concerts.

In 1875, a group of citizens, under the chairmanship of John George McCarthy, MP and local historian, formed the Great and Royal Opera House Co. and purchased the Munster Hall from Scanlan. At the same time music as a cultural element in the city began to be developed on a professional level. Opera was hugely popular amongst Corkonians.

C.J. Phipps of London was commissioned to transform the building and Munster Hall was soon transformed with the addition of two balconies and a very fine stage. The decorations of the theatre were entrusted to architect M. Edward Bell of London.

The Opera House opened on 17 September 1877 with a performance of H.J. Byron's comedy, *Our Boys* by William Duck and his company and went on to have a long and illustrious career as Cork's principal theatre. The first manager of Cork Opera House, James Scanlan, operated under a board of directors acting on behalf of a private limited company that had been formed. Fundraising events were common in the 1880s. Scanlon tried everything to raise funds, including a balloon ascent from the Cornmarket. During this event, the balloon, which had refused to ascend for the first two days, suddenly decided to do so with the result that two prominent Cork citizens were taken away in the balloon by the wind and had to walk home from Carrigtwohill. The company that was formed in 1877 went into liquidation in 1888 and a fresh group of enthusiasts formed a new company with capital of £12,000. This was the company, which through all the trials and tribulations was still in existence when the theatre burned down sixty-seven years later, in 1955. Cork Opera House was reopened with a new look in October 1965.

BARRACKA AND BUTTERA BANDS

In the late nineteenth century there were four fife and drum bands in the city, and several brass and reed, not to mention the pipe bands. The Barrack Street Band, affectionately known as the 'Barracka', was founded as a temperance band by Fr Theobald Mathew in 1837. During the early years, the band, which was the main attraction of his Temperance Society, was situated at 1 Barrack Street. When weather permitted, the band would march the ill-paved, gas-lit thoroughfares of Cork by night, playing inspirational airs, accompanied by a large following of temperance supporters parading in torchlight procession in order to give hope to those who had lost their way.

As the years rolled by, the band and its society became one of the strongest temperance and politically motivated institutes in Ireland. They achieved musical excellence due to the training and guidance of the military bandsmen from the nearby military barracks, Elizabeth Fort, and they went on to win many brass and reed band contests. Since its foundation, the Barrack Street Band has become an integral part of the cultural fabric of Cork and has continued to make a significant contribution to musical life of the city.

The Butter Exchange Band has been playing in Cork since 1878. Its name, affectionately shortened in Cork style to 'the Buttera', derives from its sponsorship by workers of the Butter Exchange, which was one of the group of fine old buildings which formed the commercial centre of the north side of the city. In 1878, the band was known as Fr Hurley's Band, after the curate who started it for the boys of Eason's Hill School, near the top of Shandon Street. On Fr Hurley's leaving, the band was taken over by the employees at the Exchange, many of whom had sons playing in it. The association continued while the boys became men, so it was not long before the band outgrew its schoolboy image and became a great source of pride to the city. Since the 1970s, the band has admitted female members. In recent years, there has been an increase in the numbers of young people in the band and it has reverted to being primarily a young person's band. The band's rehearsal rooms are located at 48 Dominick Street near the old Butter Market.

CALLANAN'S VIEWING TOWER

In the southern suburbs off Barrack Street and Tower Street, overlooking the city centre, one particularly interesting business venture was opened in 1865, that of a large tower and formal gardens owned by Michael Callanan, a city merchant. The idea for such a project grew out of Callanan's quest for wealth and he was inspired by the Crystal Palace Exhibition in London, which he visited in 1851. Here, an English arboretical architect, Sir Joseph Paxton, designed a stylistic glass building to house the Hyde Park exhibition of that year.

Three years later in 1854, the London structure was removed, extensively enlarged and set up permanently in the township of Sydenham, just south of London. Exhibitions, concerts, conferences and sporting events were held at the Crystal Palace until it was completely destroyed through fire in 1936. In the hope of making money, Callanan built a similar substantial entertainment complex on a smaller scale in Cork with a high limestone tower as the central point, instead of Paxton's glass complex.

The estimated cost of the scheme was £50,000. Ornamental gardens were designed and the tall tower was constructed approximately, 25 to 30 metres in height, which assumed the shape of a medieval tall castle. With over 100 steps to the top and crenellated at the top, the tower provided panoramic views of the city.

Once the initial gardens and tower were in place, Callanan attempted to attract the finances of others by placing large advertisements in local street directories and newspapers. Callanan detailed several attractions that he proposed to build, the majority of which were never constructed. The surrounding 'pleasure' grounds around the tower were to comprise an area of 3 hectares. Walks were to extend for about a mile in length. Callanan detailed that here 'pure bracing air' could be thoroughly enjoyed like the environment of the countryside, the advantage being that this amenity was just minutes' walk from the city. Callanan mentioned that a new and spacious concert hall was due to be built and was to be opened by July 1872 (it never was).

Rustic seats, summer-houses, fountains and grottos, were to be distributed about the grounds. The grounds were to provide space for athletic sports, gymnastics, and Olympic-type games. Archery and cricket grounds were provided, trapeze, dumb-bells and all the appliances of an open-air gymnasium supplied. Callanan stated that he gained much pleasure in directing the attention of 'amateurs and gentlemen to the facilities which his establishment offered for the practice of such games as Cricket, Lawn Billiards, Croquet, American and English Bowls, Quoits, and all the newest and most fashionable sports'. In 1871, Callanan proposed to construct a racket court and ball alley. These developments also did not occur. An extensive racecourse was proposed and laid down in lawn grass and afforded a level run of nearly half-a-mile. Callanan stated that it was his intention to occasionally produce pyrotechnic displays and to devise entertainments, which would introduce some of the choicest resources of the polytechnic art.

In the 1871 advertisement, Callanan begged to remind citizens that the tower was erected by him for the sole benefit of the sick poor of the city. Entrance to the tower was free and all classes of people were welcomed. For the satisfaction of all parties, an arrangement was made by placing a Protestant and a Roman Catholic relief box at the entrance of the tower, accessible only to the officers of the respective communities.

However, by Guy's street directory of Cork in 1875-6, the tower gardens were vacant and closed. Oral tradition has it that the place attracted too many undesirables and many foreign sailors from the ships visiting the port held drinking sessions in the area. A unnamed parish priest of St FinBarr's South intervened to stop the situation getting worse sometime between 1871 and 1875 As a result, many of the facilities and buildings were taken down, apart from the viewing tower. Today, the tower is still a prominent landmark on the south side of the city and forms a backdrop to the gardens behind the former Tower Bar on Tower Street. The formal gardens are long gone and what remains is the external shell of the tower, with over a dozen windows to be seen.

THE ART OF THE TURKISH BATH

The inventor of the Roman-Irish bath was our own Dr Richard Barter (1802-1870), of Cooldaniel, County Cork. The crumbling remains of his hydropathic baths at St Ann's, near Blarney, are gradually returning to nature. On that site, in 1856, Dr Barter built the first Turkish bath in Britain or Ireland.

Dr Barter was a popular and talented physician, who observed that drinking water enabled cholera patients to sweat and eased their symptoms. He examined a trend in European alternative medicine, the water cure. Its Czech pioneer, Vincenz Priessnitz, administered cold water to confront a range of conditions. One of his techniques was the blanket wrap: a patient was tightly wrapped in blankets and given cold water to drink. The patient was then unwrapped and sponged down with tepid water. Barter started his project with vapour baths, into which the patient sat, leaving the head exposed. Barter built a vapour-filled room, where patients could be exposed to 15 degrees Celsius more heat than the box bath generated.

St Ann's continued to treat patients in this way, until, in 1856, having read a description of Turkish baths in a book, *The Pillars of Hercules*, Dr Barter invited its author, David Urquhart, to come to St Ann's and build one for him. Turkish baths envelope the bather in steam-laden air. Forcing a muck-sweat out of his patients was central to Dr Barter's treatment, but the air in his first Turkish bath was so moist that it restricted perspiration. It, and a second bath, were judged failures and the doctor turned his attention away from the moisture-laden Turkish bath to the dry air of the baths of ancient Rome.

Dr Barter embarked on lecture tours and was involved in building bath houses, for medical and recreational use, in Cork, Dublin and elsewhere. In Cork City, a Barter Turkish baths was established on Grenville Place.

JACOB'S ON THE MALL

Another Turkish baths was sited next to the Bank of Ireland, on the Mall. Alf Jacobs's Cork Turkish Bath Co. started planning the conversion of an already existing building in 1890. The main work was carried out by E. & P. O'Flynn to the design of the architect, Arthur Hill. The gas and general plumbing work was undertaken by M. Barry, and the painting and decoration by J.S. McCarthy.

Because the bricks and tiles had to be manufactured specially for the project, there was considerable delay in completing the work. But from what can still be seen of the building today, we must assume that Jacobs thought the delay worthwhile when, on Saturday 17 October 1891, he was finally able to open for business. Certainly the *Irish Builder* thought them worthy of description. The entrance to the baths was through a tiled passage executed, as was all the tiling, by Nicholas Sisk. The passage is still in use today, and currently leads to Jacobs on the Mall, a restaurant named after the original managing director of the baths.

At the end of the passage was the Turkish bath ticket office. After paying the admission charge, the bather left any valuables in one of a series of lockers and was given a key.

The first of the main rooms in the Turkish bath was a large 18m by 12m cooling-room, maintained at between 52°C and 60°C. During daylight hours, natural light filtered through softly tinted glass in the high ceiling. At the northern end of the room was a gallery set aside for smokers. Around the cooling-room were individual cubicles, upholstered and screened, for bathers to undress in and leave their clothes – enough, it was claimed, to cater for fifty bathers at a time.

Along the centre of the room, was an oval plunge bath, 8m by 2½m, with a minimum depth of 1m. There were three hot rooms, each lined with ornamental brickwork and tiling. The first, only slightly hotter than the cooling-room, was 7m by 10m. The second was in the shape of an elongated octagon, 3½m by 9m, maintained at a temperature of 71°C to 82°C. Finally, there was an inner room where 'those who can stand it can breathe a temperature of from 250 to 300 degrees [121 to 149°C]'.

Unlike Barter's Turkish baths, in which the required room temperatures were maintained by hot air passing through an underfloor hypocaust, Jacobs used what was known as the Bartholomew system. Fresh air was drawn into the building and then heated by being passed over a stove. It then passed directly through the hot rooms, starting with the hottest and cooling as it passed into the other rooms.

It has been suggested that the Turkish baths were closed down during an outbreak of polio in the city in 1943 and that the Bishop of Cork refused to allow them to be re-opened, but the evidence is unclear. There is a certain irony here in that in the aftermath of the poliomyelitis epidemic which hit Cork in the summer of 1956, the building was converted into an aftercare centre known as the 'Polio Clinic'. New equipment was installed and physiotherapy and swimming facilities were made available to help rehabilitate those who had suffered during the last years before Jonas Salk's discovery of the first polio vaccine. Though the Turkish baths have long since disappeared, the building, which is now the home of a well-thought-of restaurant, has again become a place to visit with one's friends for enjoyable relaxation, albeit in somewhat cooler surroundings.

A PLACE FOR EVERYMAN

The Everyman was designed by H. Brunton and built around 1840 by John O'Connell. Located on MacCurtain Street, this terraced two-bay three-storey building was originally constructed as a house, which was part of a group with the adjoining houses to the east and west. In 1897 Dan Lowrey opened the building as a luxurious new theatre called the Cork Palace of Varieties. Its origins as a beautiful Victorian theatre is reflected in the interior of the building with its impressive ornate proscenium arch with boxes and a balcony and ceiling composed of decorative plasterwork, which has been restored to its former glory. During the heyday of music hall theatre 1897–1912 no expense was spared in securing the best talent available at the time. Artists such as Charlie Chaplin, George Formby and Laurel and Hardy, to name a few, performed here during this time.

With the arrival of the 'talkies', the Palace became a cinema in 1930 and remained so until 1988. The venue reopened as a theatre in 1990 when it was purchased by the Everyman Theatre Company. The names of the venue and the theatre company were combined to form the Everyman Palace Theatre, but it is now known simply as 'The Everyman'.

The Everyman is now one of the busiest presenting and producing theatres in Ireland, playing host to production companies as well as diverse acts such as Ed Harris, Tommy Tiernan, Rosaleen Linehan, Glen Hansard and Marketa

Irglova. It incorporates a diverse and eclectic programme of world-class theatre, dance, music, visual arts, family entertainment and variety shows. The Everyman specialises in drama and receives regular visits from companies such as Druid, Blue Raincoat, The Abbey, Second Age and London Classic Theatre.

THE WORLD FAIR

Perhaps the key event of the first ten years of the twentieth century in Cork was the Cork International Exhibition. Large-scale exhibitions were not new to the city. The first major exhibition was held in 1852 and the second in 1883. Perhaps what started the citizens of Cork thinking once again of holding an exhibition was the one that was held in Paris in 1900. The the inception of the 1902 project has been credited to Edward Fitzgerald, who was Lord Mayor of Cork in 1901.

The opening day in May 1902 was observed as a general holiday. The large drapery houses remained closed till 2 p.m., by which time the procession had passed through the thoroughfares. From an early hour, people anxious to watch the spectacle crowded every vantage point. Special trains ran on all the railway systems converging on the city.

Henry A. Cutler designed the General Exhibition Buildings while Honorary Architect William O'Connell, Hanover Street, Cork, a well-known local builder, constructed all the buildings, halls, kiosks, and restaurants. The largest of the buildings was

The central ground at the Cork International Exhibition, 1902. (Unknown artist, archives, Cork City Museum)

approached by a flight of steps of Irish stone, on which were raised four columns surmounted with Corinthian caps, and lead to the Grand Avenue. The whole building was surmounted by a dome, which was embellished with four corner turrets and a cupola. The industrial hall, made of fibrous plaster, had a floor space of 170,000 square feet (51,816 square metres) and comprised seven parallel avenues and one avenue at right angles.

Several hundred exhibits were on display from May to October. With such a display, extensive regulations existed for exhibitors. The charge inside the building was two shillings per square foot. Exhibits were not admitted until payment for space had been made in full. The main categories of exhibits were: Women's Section, Raw Materials Section, Geological Specimens, Natural History Section, Modern Science Section, Archaeological and Historical Section, Industrially Treated Forestry, Educational Section, and Nature Study Section.

Sports of all kinds took place on the Sports Grounds, where a 'grand stand' was provided. The sports included athletic and bicycle contests, lawn tennis tournaments, crickets and other minor sports. On the River Lee, which flowed beside the Exhibition Gardens, electric launches, gondolas, and ferries frequently plied. On the other side of the river were the pretty gardens of Sunday's Well. Gondolas were steered by Venetian boatmen, who entertained the passengers by singing songs of Ireland. A Great Water Chute was constructed close to the Industrial Hall, and measured 21m in height. Cars carried passengers up a gradual ascent to the summit, when a seat was taken in one of the boats, which then started down the incline, hitting the water at speed. There was also a Skating Rink, Picture Gallery and The Cave of the Winds, set in a Rocky cavern near the Lee.

By the close of the exhibition of 1902, over 1 million people had visited the Mardyke. It was decided, therefore, to run it again the following year. The official opening of the renamed 1903 Greater Cork International Exhibition occurred on Thursday, 28 May 1903 when the Lord Lieutenant of Ireland, the Earl of Dudley, officially opened the event. During the run of the exhibition, King Edward VII visited it. After the final close on 31 October 1903, work commenced on the demolition of the exhibition buildings which were eventually auctioned off.

In March 1906, it was agreed to vest the park and Shrubberies House in Cork Corporation with the proviso that the corporation would levy a rate of a halfpenny in the pound for the annual upkeep and maintenance. A further proviso stipulated that the Shrubberies House would be used by the Corporation as a municipal museum. Fitzgerald's Park was born.

DOWN THE SHOWGROUNDS

For over 160 years, the Cork Show was the most important annual event in the city's calendar. From 1857 till 1890 the shows of the County of Agricultural Society were held in the ground of the Corn Market. In a lecture given to commemorate the centenary of the society in 1957, Captain Denis Gould, secretary of the society, quoted from a catalogue of an agricultural show held in July 1860 at which horse, sheep, poultry, dairy produce, cattle and implements were shown. The cattle shown were Ayshires, Shorthorns, Herefords, West Highlands, Kerrys, Angus, Galloway and Dutch. There were sixty-nine trade stands and the machinery included a combined mill for crushing or bruising oats, linseed, malt and barley, and splitting beans and peas. An attachment provided for the splitting or grinding of beans.

From 1892 the County of Cork Agricultural Society developed its new home in the Cork Park Racecourse. It was dependent on the success of its shows and the subscriptions and voluntary contributions of its members. They worked in close association with the Department of Agriculture and the County Cork Committee of Agriculture and received grants from them for prize funds. Recognising the society's links with wider Munster agricultural bodies, in 1908 the name of the County of Cork Agricultural Society was changed to the Munster Agricultural Society.

The creation of Cork City Council's South Docklands plan brought further changes to the Munster Agricultural Society. The Council's compulsory purchase order meant that in July 2009, for the first time in its history, the Cork Summer Show was held outside the city. A 24ha site, just off the Ballincollig

Bypass, became the new home for the Munster Agricultural Society's two-day show.

CINEMAS ON ST PATRICK'S STREET

The Pavilion Cinema opened on Thursday, 10 March 1921 with a single presentation of D.W. Griffith's epic, *The Greatest Question*. The interior was impressive, consisting of a plush 900-seat auditorium fitted with comfortable cushioned seats. The Tallon family from the Rochestown Road were the owners of this new cinema, and Fred Harford was the first manager. It was the finest cinema in the city with an extensive orchestral music area to accompany the silent films. The 'talkies' made their debut on Monday 5 August 1928 with an Al Jolson film, *The Singing Fool*. The film caused a huge stir in Cork and drew in 12,000 people in the first five days alone. The 'Pav' had a contract to show all the MGM films. The auditorium also had a stage on which live shows, recitals and concerts were frequently held, to great popular acclaim.

On 16 February 1930, disaster struck when a fire swept through the building. The Pavilion was severely gutted but it reopened, fully remodelled and redecorated, the following June. The building also possessed a fashionable restaurant and was always a suitable place to take a first date. The restaurant was often used for workshops during the Film Festival. Spiralling costs led to the closure of the famous restaurant in 1985. The Pavilion closed in August of 1989 with a screening of *Indiana Jones and the Last Crusade* as its final film.

The Savoy Cinema was constructed in the early 1930s. It was commissioned by the Rank Organisation, and was built by the firm of Meaghar and Hayes. The first film was shown on Thursday, 12 May 1932. The cinema had a colourful art deco exterior with an imposing exterior lighted canopy. The interior design was elaborate with a spacious marble foyer. The rear of the Grand Circle was known as the Gods, which was the cheapest part of the house. The grand auditorium held an audience of 2,249 patrons. The Studios of Rank, United Artists, 20th Century Fox and Columbia supplied new films to the Savoy and the programme changed twice a week on Sundays and Wednesdays.

Sunday was always 'the' night of the week to go to the pictures when people dressed in their best clothes. Fred Bridgeman was the organist, and was the Savoy's top live entertainer for nearly thirty years. The Cork Film International Festival, originally called 'An Tostal', began in 1953. For one week each year, the Savoy was home to the festival. By 1970, the character of the Savoy was starting to fade. The departure of Fred Bridgeman signalled the end of the era of the cinema organ and the grand sing-a-long shows. In July 1973, the Savoy cinema closed. Today, part of the Savoy is a shopping centre and the remainder is awaiting redevelopment.

9

THE SPORTING CITY

ROWING PROWESS

The oldest rowing club in Cork is the Lee Rowing Club, which was founded in 1850. The first boat club was on Albert Quay (now MacSwiney Quay). After a fire in 1880 a boat club was built near the Lower Glanmire Road and in 1886 the club moved to the present site on the Marina. The top half of the clubhouse, except for the roof, was one of the exhibition halls used during the Cork Exhibition on 1902. The original roof was replaced in 1939.

The club's nickname was the 'collars and cuffs' because many of its members were apprentice tailors. It was associated with Lees GAA Club and had the same colours, red and black. The club's greatest triumphs came in 1925 and 1933 when it won the Leander trophy. In July 1890 the club asked the great Charles Stewart Parnell for a financial contribution to help clear their debts. Parnell obliged and he was made an honorary member of the club.

Although the Shandon Boat Club was founded in May 1877, its lineage stretches back to the beginning of organised competitive amateur rowing in Cork twenty years earlier. In 1858 Cork Harbour Rowing Club (CHRC), was founded. Ten years later, in 1868, Queens College Rowing Club was founded by a number of members who left CHRC after a dispute and nine years later that club changed its name to Shandon Boat Club, due to the lack of 'college men' rowing with the club by that time.

In 1871 the Cork City Council granted land to Queens College Rowing Club to build a boathouse on the Navigation Wall of the Marina and this boathouse was knocked down in

1896 and replaced by the building still in use today. The new building was designed by the well-known Cork architect, James McMullen, who also designed the Honan Chapel in University College Cork. Following its foundation the club thrived and in a few short years became one of the strongest clubs in Irish rowing, winning on many occasions at the Metropolitan Regatta in Dublin (then the equivalent of the Irish National Championships). W.D. Thornton, 'Ireland's greatest oarsman' according to *The Irish Times*, was stroke of the Shandon crews during its early years.

Cork Boat Club had its first outing at Cobh Regatta in 1899 when it had its first successes. In 1902 at the International Regatta at the Marina a Junior VII was successful against eight other crews. The spectators were so enthralled by this success that a massive collection was taken up and allowed the committee to rent the old Coastguard premises at Undercliffe Blackrock, which remains the club's home to the present day. The original Boat House was a pavilion from the Cork International Exhibition and housed the clubs boats and equipment until 1939. The old Coastguard building was converted into dressing rooms and club rooms fronted by well laid out gardens and a beautiful lawn on which band prom-enades every weekend considerably helped club funds. The club's first major success was in 1905 when the Leander Ship was won for the first time. This trophy had been presented in 1904 by the Leander Rowing Club in appreciation for the wonderful hospi-tality they had received from the citizens and Regatta Committee and Trinity were the first winners of the trophy.

AGAINST THE WICKET

Founded in 1849 as the Cork Cricket Club, the 'County' was added to it in 1874. In its 140-year history, the Mardyke has hosted thirteen international fixtures, the first in 1902 against a London County team featuring W.G. Grace, Australian captain Bill Murdoch and future England captain J.H.T. Douglas, and the most recent in 2002 against an MCC side over three days. Test players such as Graham Gouch, Nasir Hussain, Peter

Such, Derek Pringle and John Stephenson have all graced the Mardyke over recent decades. One of the significant changes to club teams was during the First World War. Touring teams did not come but there was plenty of cricketing activity as there were large numbers of naval and military personnel based in the area. In 1922, when Ireland became independent, the military departed and the club became more dependent on local leagues, annual inter-provincials against Leinster and visits from teams such as Trinity College and Na Shulers (an Irish Touring Club).

THE SECOND GAA MEETING

Gaelic games represented everything Irish and represented a cultural identity that was passed down through time, empowering each generation. The idea for the GAA was posed by Michael Cusack who was born in Carron, County Clare, in 1847. A fascinating and complex personality, his passion for Gaelic games was matched only by his love of the unique and beautiful Burren limestone landscape where he was born and raised. He had a love of teaching and after nearly twenty years' experience in different schools he set up his own academy at 4 Gardiners Place in Dublin in 1878. He also had an active interest in athletics. In 1879, he was the All-Ireland champion at putting 16lb shot and again in 1882. He deemed that athletic contests needed to encompass more people, as under the present rules it was confined to the gentry, the military and the middle class, with artisans and labourers excluded.

Michael Cusack also approached Archbishop Thomas Croke of Caiseal who was a strong supporter of Irish nationalism. He had aligned himself with the Irish National Land League during the Land War, and with the chairman of the Irish Parliamentary Party, Charles Stewart Parnell. Maurice Davin, another ally that Michael Cusack recruited, was an outstanding athlete who won international fame in the 1870s when he held numerous world records for running, hurdling, jumping and weight-throwing. He was actively campaigning for a body to control Irish athletics from 1877. He gave his support to Cusack's campaign from the summer of 1884.

The name for his new organisation that Cusack first proposed was the Munster Athletic Club. The first meeting was initially supposed to be in Cork. Hurling was widely played around Cork City at the time, with teams such as St Finbarr's, Blackrock, Ballygarvan, Ballinhassig and Cloghroe in regular opposition in challenge contests. However, due to its location, Thurles was chosen and a new name came to fruition, the Gaelic Athletic Association. The meeting was held on 1 November 1884 with the object of reviving native pastimes such as hurling, football according to Irish rules, running, jumping, weight throwing and other athletic pastimes of an Irish character, which were in danger of extinction

Those that attended the first meeting were Michael Cusack, Maurice Davin (who presided), John Wyse Power (editor of the *Leinster Leader*), John McKay (a journalist with the *Cork Examiner*), T.K. Bracken (a builder from Templemore), P.J. Ryan (a solicitor from Callan) and Thomas St George McCarthy (an athlete and member of the RIC).

Eleven days after the establishment of the new organisation, the first athletic meeting under its auspices was held in Toames, near Macroom. A second meeting to help develop the ideas of the GAA was held in the Victoria Hotel, Cork, on 27 December 1884. The meeting had letters before it from Davitt, Parnell and Dr Croke accepting the invitations to become patrons. Through the following two years, a Cork County Board was formed.

From mid-summer 1892, the County of Cork Agricultural Society decided to rent out the new grounds to interested groups. One of the first groups to hire the jumping ground was the Church of Ireland Association, Cycle Club. It was for their sports day. It was also decided to allow their competitors to train on the track for a week beforehand as long as it did not interfere with any other activities. Other groups at that time that rented out the space were the Cork Cycle Club, Cork Athletic Club, United Football Club, the Gaelic Athletic Association, the Irish Automobile Club and the Cork Gun Club.

Fast forward to 1976 and Páirc Uí Chaoimh opened. It was named after Pádraig Ó Caoimh, who was a native of Cork and was general secretary of the GAA between 1929-1964. In 2014, planning permission was passed to create a new modern stadium.

Twenty-five clubs, divisions and colleges currently participate in the Hurling Cork County Championship. The title has been won at least once by nineteen different clubs. The all-time record-holders are Blackrock National Hurling Club, who have led the roll of honour since the competition's inception and have won a total of thirty-two titles. Nemo Rangers top the Cork Senior Football Championship on a record eighteen occasions.

Cork possesses thirty All-Ireland Senior Hurling Championships with six All-Ireland Senior Football Championships. In 2014, the Cork women's senior camogie team and the women's senior football team won their respective All-Ireland cups. Twenty-five clubs, divisions and colleges currently participate in the Cork County Championship.

THE GREATEST HURLER

Christy Ring. (Unknown photographer, archives, Cork City Library)

Nicholas Christopher Ring (1920-1979), better known as Christy Ring, was a famous Irish sportsman. He played hurling with the famous Glen Rovers club from 1941 until 1967 and was a member of the Cork senior team from 1939 until 1963. He is widely regarded as one of the greatest hurlers in the history of the game. Many former players, commentators and fans place him as the number one player of all-time.

Christy Ring's status as one of the all-time greats is self-evident. His record of sixty-four appearances in championship games has yet to be equalled, while his tally of thirty-three goals and 208 points in these games was a record score that stood until the 1970s. Christy's haul of eight senior All-Ireland medals, all won on the field of play, was a record which stood for over a decade. Christy also won a record eighteen Railway Cup medals with Munster. No other player in the history of the competition has gone into double figures.

TENNIS BY THE LEE

Sunday's Well Boating and Tennis Club was founded in 1899, shortly after a successful July 'Sunday's Well Regatta and Water Carnival' had been held on the Lee. The club was formed by some of the regatta committee organisers, who were boating and tennis enthusiasts from the locality. The committee then leased a plot of ground off the Mardyke Walk alongside the river and that is the ground which the club occupies today. As a club, Sunday's Well is fortunate in that it can boast of having a comprehensive range of annals dating from its foundation right up to present times. It was uniquely linked with the Cork International Exhibition of 1902/03, principally because it lent its grounds to the exhibition, and the present clubhouse was built by the Exhibition Committee for visiting dignitaries, which included King Edward VII and Queen Alexandra.

In 1904, the club took possession of the clubhouse, and according to records, a firm of architects employed by the Sunday's Well committee reported that: 'the estimated useful life of the clubhouse was less than 30 years'. It is interesting to note that in 1984, another firm of architects estimated the life of the same building to be – yes, you've guessed it – not less than thirty years. After that Cork Exhibition, Sunday's Well had, in addition to its magnificent new clubhouse, five excellently laid out and perfectly manicured grass courts. These, set in peaceful and beautiful surroundings, became the pride of the county. Throughout the summer, the courts were constantly used from morning to night, except on band promenade days, which were held regularly during the summer months in front of the clubhouse.

IRISH INTERNATIONAL RUGBY

Cork Constitution did not have a ground in the early days and the first recorded playing venue was at the Old Cork Park Racecourse, which later became the industrial site where Henry Ford & Son established their tractor and motor car assembly plant. The club also played in Blackrock, on ground adjacent to H.L. Tivy's home at Barnstead, Church Road.

In 1897, the club took a tenancy on the ground known as Johnny Butler's Field at Turner's Cross and laid out the ground that is now owned by the Munster Football Association. Soccer and Gaelic games were played there, as well as rugby and it was the venue for Munster Cup and senior interprovincials until 1904. The club left there and passed their tenancy to the Cork Football Company. They spent a season at a ground near the Lough and another season at the Showgrounds in Ballintemple, courtesy of the Munster Agricultural Society.

The Cork Exhibition was held at the Mardyke in 1902-1903 and afterwards a few enterprising businessmen set up the Cork Football Company to redevelop the Mardyke site as a sporting area. The group included Alderman P.H. Meade, a member of Constitution and a former mayor, and John Reese, a turf accountant and owner of Civility Stud Farm on the South Douglas Road. They raised £2,500 and set out the grounds that are now the UCC grounds, and purchased the Tudor-style building that served as the clubhouse in the early years. Constitution and Cork County were the first tenants and played each other in the first game at the venue in September 1904. Ireland played England at the ground in 1905 and it became the home of Munster Rugby until 1954.

However, the Grounds Company struggled financially and eventually the site was bought out by University College Cork with the assistance of the Irish Rugby Football Union and through the funding of Professor Alexander, a former IRFU President. The Union advanced a loan of £775 to UCC to purchase the leasehold and the college became the new owners. In December 1912 the college and Constitution clubs became the sole tenants on a £25 per year lease until 1912. The Munster Branch and the Cork Clubs had playing rights for a percentage of gate receipts. There were occasions over the years when Constitution were in arrears to UCC and UCC to the Union, but they struggled on.

In 1950, the 1912 agreement expired and UCC gave Constitution notice with a two-year extension granted. UCC did not renew the agreement. By then the Munster Branch had acquired Musgrave Park and it came into operation in the 1954/55 season. Meanwhile Constitution had sourced a new ground at Temple Hill. Constitution's last Munster game at the Mardyke was against Dolphin in 1954, and Munster's last game was against the All Blacks, also in that year.

Great players have emerged over the years and ended up being leaders of Irish rugby squads such as Ronan O'Gara, Peter Stringer and Ken Murphy. They won the first EU tournament in the South of France with Peter Stringer and Ronan O'Gara as the half backs. In terms of important rugby players, there have been eighteen that have played international and at Lions level. Peter O'Mahony and Simon Zebo are two on the national rugby team now.

FORDSON FOOTBALL TEAM

The Fordson Football team played in the League of Ireland between 1924 and hold a record that can never be bettered. The club was originally the factory team of the Ford Motor Company, a major employer in the city at that time and was named after the Fordson tractor, resulting in the nickname 'The Tractors'. In 1924 Fordsons were runners-up in the FAI Cup, losing 1-0 to Athlone Town. Later that year, they were admitted to the League of Ireland, replacing Midland Athletic. As a result they became the first ever club from Cork to play in the league.

Their finest hour came on St Patrick's Day in 1926 when they won the FAI Cup, defeating Shamrock Rovers in Dublin by 3 goals to 2. It was the first time the cup had come to Cork. The team was given a hero's welcome on their return to the city. Incidentally, Fordson Football Team home grounds were where Pic-du-Jer Park is now located. In 1928, when the Irish Free State beat Belgium 4-2 in an away game, the team featured four Fordson players – Paddy Barry, Charlie Dowdall, Jack O'Sullivan and John Wade. Sullivan scored the last goal with a penalty in the 79th minute. This was the first penalty to be scored at international level by an Irish player. In 1930 Ford ended its association with the club. The club continued to play under several different names, including Cork City FC, Cork United and Cork Athletic until the 1950s.

CORK'S SON OF SOCCER

Cork has produced many noble and distinguished soccer sons, but in the annals of the English ball game, Roy Keane has carved a special place for himself in the breath-taking world of soccer superstars. In his eighteen-year playing career, he played for Cobh Ramblers, Nottingham Forest and Manchester United, before ending his career at Celtic. He played at international level for much of his career, representing the Republic of Ireland over a period of fourteen years, most of which he spent as captain. He played in every Republic of Ireland game at the 1994 FIFA World Cup, although he was sent home from the 2002 World Cup after an incident with national coach Mick McCarthy. He was appointed manager of Sunderland shortly after his retirement as a player. In April 2009, he was appointed as manager of Ipswich Town. In November 2013, he was appointed assistant manager of the Republic of Ireland national football team by manager Martin O'Neill.

FIGHTING HARD AND FAIR

There are twenty-four boxing clubs in the city and county. One of Cork's earliest champions was Jack McAuliffe. He was lightweight champion of the world from 1886 to 1896. He was undefeated for a total of thirteen years in the USA. He was originally from Christ Church Lane, off South Main Street. His family emigrated to the USA when he was six years old. He started boxing in the USA as a young lad and had won over 200 fights as an amateur before turning professional.

On the professional front, there is Gary Hyde, who manages a number of World Champions and Gary 'Spike' O'Sullivan, WBO International middleweight champion. Talented Cork amateur boxers currently include Dave Roche, bronze medallist world champion, Rory O'Donoghue and heavyweight Pat O'Shea.

KING OF THE ROAD

Mick Barry occupied an unparalleled place in the sport of road bowling. In 2010 Cork City Council named a road in his honour. University College Cork, where he worked as head gardener, honoured him with an honorary degree and he was named Supreme Bowler of the Millennium by Ból-Chumann na hÉireann in 1999. From 1962 until 1975 he was Munster Senior champion in all but three years. He twice completed a four in-a-row, from 1964 to 1967 and 1969 to 1972. For a team that would be incredible, but he had to do it on his own in a highly competitive sport where one mistake could signal defeat.

Barry returned to active competition in the 1990s, winning three Munster Vintage (over-sixty) finals, the most famous being his 1994 win over his great rival Denis O'Donovan at Crossbarry. At seventy-five years of age he covered the road in eighteen shots, better than the majority of players could do at twenty-five. The sport is littered with his records, like putting a 16oz bowl over the Chetwynd Viaduct, lofting Mary Anne's pub on Dublin Hill ... it goes on and on. He did things that didn't seem humanly possible. But more importantly he did those things with a level of integrity equally supreme.

TRACK HEROES

Cork has had and has several track champions. Sonia O'Sullivan began her running career in Ballymore Running Club which is located in the eastern side of Cobh town. She was one of the world's leading female 5,000m runners for most of the 1990s and early 2000s. Her crowning achievement was a gold medal in the 5,000m at the 1995 World Athletics Championships.

She won silver medals in the 5,000m at the 2000 Olympic Games and in the 1,500m at the 1993 World Championships. She also won three European Championship gold medals and two World Cross-Country Championship gold medals.

Derval O'Rourke is an Irish former sprint hurdles athlete. She competed internationally in the 60 and 100m hurdles, and is the Irish national record holder in both events. She participated in two Indoor World Championships, the last five Outdoor World Championships and the 2004, 2008, and 2012 Summer Olympics.

Rob Heffernan is an Irish race walker. At the 2008 Olympic Games he came eighth in the 20km walk. His wife Marian Andrews is also national women's 400m champion and was on the Irish women's team that finished fourth in the European indoors. On 27 July 2010, Heffernan won the bronze medal in the 2010 European Athletics Championships in the 20km walk. At the 2012 Olympics, Heffernan finished ninth in the 20km race. A week later he finished fourth in the 50km, finishing seven minutes faster than the previous national record. His two performances were the top two performances for the Irish Athletics team at the 2012 Olympics. On 14 August 2013, Heffernan finished first in the 2013 World Championships in the athletics 50km event in Moscow, finishing over a minute clear of the silver medal position with a winning time. The winning time was the fastest time in the world in 2013 by more than three minutes.

Also from The History Press

IRELAND AT WAR